My Name Means FAITH

A Memoir of Spiritual Awakening
through Maitreya, the Friend of All Souls

Shraddha Friend

My Name Means FAITH
Copyright © 2025 Shraddha Friend

All rights reserved.

ISBN 979-8-9927312-0-0 (paperback)
ISBN 979-8-9927312-1-7 (ebook)

Book Design: Clarity Designworks

Maitreya's Morning First Prayer

My God! My Beloved! My own True Self!

I surrender completely unto Thee! Restore Thy Authority!

Manifest Thy Presence within this little self until it has become One with Thee, shining forth with Thy Own Clear Light! Let me know, this moment, my Oneness with Thee; the one thing I lack; through which all else is made Perfect!

Heal the division in me; that I may Know Thy Oneness in all this that is! Consume this little self in the Sacred Fire of Thy Presence! That I may find my way through the Ordeal and be Liberated from it, Realizing my Oneness with Thee!

From the unreal, lead me to The Real!

From darkness, lead me to the Light!

From division, lead me to Wholeness!

From the temporary, lead me to The Eternal!

From death, lead me to Immortality!

O Beloved God! I would be One with Thee fully this moment!

Make my Doing One with my Speech!

Make my Speech One with my Mind!

Make my Mind One with my Heart!

Make my Heart One with my Will!

And my Will One with Thy Will!

Shatter this prison of false self; and absorb me, in the Ocean of Your Infinite Divine Being, as a drop of water in the Sea! That I shall know, without doubt or reservation that You and I are not we, but One! For Thou art my only True Self;

Majestic! Splendorous! Immortal! There is no I but Thee! So be it with me!

The Friend of All Souls, Maitreya.
The Holy Book of Destiny (p. 194). Kindle Edition.

Table of Contents

Acknowledgements

First and foremost, I am forever indebted to Adhyatma Bhaga-van Sri Babajhan Al-Kahlil The Friend of All Souls through the Grace of the One Universal God.

I am beyond grateful to Tara Friend, Shanti Friend and Ila Friend. Their patience and guidance helped bring my dreams to reality. Our bond with all Maitreyians will never be broken.

To all my friends and family, named and unnamed, for being there for me on all my journeys.

A special thank you to Christina Sussmann, the first editor who took my stream of consciousness and made it into a "real book".

And to a remarkable young woman, Amanda Peck, whose creativity, insight and editorial assistance remains invaluable.

We are all One in Spirit. My Faith knows no bounds.

Introduction

Here Goes My Oughtabiography:

All the things I've done with my life,
and those that I am still working toward

What is your purpose in life? What a loaded question to begin with, I know. But, seriously, have you ever thought about it? I mean, really thought about why you're here on this earth, right this moment. What if I could tell you with absolute certainty that I know the purpose of life? What if you could experience the Truth of your Oneness with Universal God through your own direct and personal experience? Even more so, what if you could turn your experience around and give that true Gift to others. As Maitreya the Friend said, "A closed mind is a very dark place." So, open your mind. Open your heart, and experience this as yourself, as your True Nature. If you ask for God, you get God, not something other than God. You don't need to take my word for the truth; you can find out for yourself through your own experience.

Around 2010, I walked around Hermosa Beach Pier with a clipboard and asked random people a series of questions, including, "*Do you believe it's possible for a man or woman to become awakened by God in our time, in our day and age, not just in the past?*" I was delighted to find that almost 90% of the people answered, "*Yes,*" in a kind of surprised tone, like they had never asked themselves such a thing, but were pleased to come up with the typical relaxed response of, "*Well, why not?*"

My name is Shraddha, which means "Faith through Direct Experience." I've had somewhat of a difficult life with perhaps more trials and tribulations than some (although much less than others). My faith has been tested more times than I can count, but through it all, it has proven indestructible for over thirty years. My hope for this book is that through my experiences and what I have learned in my ongoing faith journey, you can experience what I know to be true. I don't want you to believe me. Because, as Maitreya often said, there is a lie in every beLIEf. But like the people I interviewed on the street, I do hope you are one of those people who can believe it is possible. And, with your heart open to all possible possibilities, you develop your own Faith through Direct Experience, just like me.

I started this memoir during Covid 2020, to reach those who are right and ready to change themselves and the world. Because I know that once a person has his or her own spiritual experience, your faith can—and will be—as certain and as indestructible as my own.

If I can promise you anything, it is that by following along with my journey while being open to your own direct experience, your life and the lives of those nearest and dearest to you will be forever changed, for the better. Will you join me?

∽♥

CHAPTER ONE

Maitreya
The Friend of All Souls

Maitreya Adhyatma Bhagavan Sri Babajhan Al-Khalil The Friend finally completed his journey on Earth and ascended to the next plane, the Spiritual Realm, on July 29, 2012. I was by his side in his final days along with my elder spiritual community. I said my regretful apologies and my goodbyes and bid farewell to the man who had changed my life immeasurably over the years, as he released his last breath.

I was glad I had these final moments with him. I knew he had been sick, but I and several of his other followers were in denial that this was really the end. If you've ever been around someone in the last stages of life, you always think you have more time. Or, that there is something that can be done; modern medicine, perhaps a miracle. Either way, we all kept hoping that there must be something we could do. Maitreya had cancer. It was prostate cancer that had spread to the liver. The kind of disease that when you're in the heart of it you think, *Oh that doesn't sound too bad.* It's only in retrospect, or from afar, that you can truly grasp that a diagnosis like that means one thing and one thing only—it's time to put away all your anger, your pettiness, the million little things you've held onto over the years and find some sort of closure before it's too late.

Nevertheless, we took turns sitting with him. There was no way that any of us were going to let him lay there alone. I'll go into it a little more later, but I'd always felt like I was on the outside of things, looking in. This experience was no different. Was I ever as close to Maitreya, as Tara or Shanti or Ila was? I guess it didn't matter anymore. As anybody who has been at somebody's deathbed before can testify, it can be one of the most incredibly beautiful honors in life. It is a heart-wrenching, soul-crushing, sad and beautiful black hole that remains a fixed point in your memory for the rest of your life. Especially when it's your friend. Your teacher. Somebody who has been there for you in the good times and the bad, who's withstood your spouts of anger and lifted you up when you were already riding high. And when it came to Maitreya, it wasn't only his death I was concerned with. It was everything he represented and had built in the world. As I sat there and watched our Spiritual Founder die, I prayed our religion wouldn't die with him.

I talked to him as we sat together and I promised Maitreya I would do all I could to help spread the word about his teachings. It was his call to Divine Critical Mass that I would not let die with him as he left this earth. This Divine Critical Mass is a moment in time when enough souls have received Maitreya's Holy Initiation, followed his teachings, and reached enlightenment alongside us, that God will spread True Enlightenment to every single soul in the universe. As I made my vow to him, Maitreya didn't say much to me, but I could tell he appreciated my promise. However, I had made vows to him before.

It's interesting the things that pass through your mind as you sit with someone as I was sitting with him. Memories flood. Good times bring a smile to your face and not so good times carry more weight than expected. Not all had been perfect in our relationship, and I felt that I owed him final apologies. It would hopefully partly clear my conscience, but also maybe ease something in his spirit as well. And so, I turned to him and apologized. I told him I was sorry. I was sorry for all the times I'd gotten angry and lashed out at him.

Maybe it was my Irish blood, my hormone issues, hypoglycemia, my rough childhood, a combination of everything, I don't know. But I knew that I had hurt Maitreya and those around me with my rage. I took responsibility for that. I'll be honest with you; this was one of the hardest things I had ever done, but with that, I finally made peace with Maitreya. Then, I waited there. And waited. And waited some more each day. Tara, Shanti, and Ila stayed with him more than I did, but I was at his bedside a few hours each day. It was a time of solace, reflection, and some slight peace. I reflected on how I never did live up to my spiritual vows as could clearly be seen from my failures.

His condition deteriorated before my eyes. Initially, he was able to walk the distance of a half block, but then in what seemed like overnight, he was only able to walk to the cafeteria. I'll always remember the two of us, mostly silent, next to each other in the elevator. And then Maitreya, being his usual self with the cafeteria workers, standing there unabashed in his hospital gown, smiling, and joking with the kitchen workers. And then, again mostly silently, taking the elevator back to his room. I stood alongside him in that elevator but his silence told me that this was his journey alone.

In a matter of days, he was barely able to walk. It was that quick. He went from holding a cup of water, to having to have it held for him, to having to have a straw in it, to finally on the last day not being able to swallow—but just asking for a little water to hold in his mouth—all in one week. He also started tapering down on the pain meds. He said he didn't want them to cloud his mind so much, like they had on a previous hospital visit.

His senses were highly alert. As his body was preparing for his transition, he would ask us not to speak so loud and finally on his last day, he asked that we not talk at all. He whispered this request to us, and we granted it. He wanted it to be peaceful, and so it was. He knew his time was drawing near.

It wasn't long after he asked for this peace that he took his final breath. As much as I thought I had prepared for this moment, it was still so unexpected and surreal. The attending nurse frantically tried to bring him back once he took his last breath, but she was unsuccessful in doing so. It was time. I was pleading, "*Is he gone? Is he really gone?*" And in that exact moment, the lights over his bed began to flicker, a lot. Before this moment, none of us had ever seen the lights flicker.

Immediately after he passed, we sang our Holy Gayatri around his bedside, and Tara anointed his forehead with our Holy Water. They let us stay in the room for a few hours. I couldn't leave. I couldn't stop holding his hand, it was still warm. I had never been so sad in my entire lifetime.

I sat by Maitreya's bed until he took his final breath and soared off. But although this would be the last time I'd ever sit next to Maitreya and communicate with him in person, this wouldn't be the last time I'd see him again—far from it. July 29, 2012, might have been The Friend's last day on Earth, but it was not the end of his life.

It is noteworthy that people across the globe were really going on about 2012 for months in 2011. New Agers kept foretelling that something was going to happen. Even mainstream news had stories about something happening in 2012. There were some explanations about this year being the end of the Mayan calendar, and possibly—and dramatically—the end of the world as we knew it. And while it was not the exact prediction, something big *did* happen. The Satya Yuga (the Age of God's Pure Truth) became fuller. The Mayans were right; it was an important year. Maitreya passed away and entered The Spiritual Realm in the middle of 2012. As he entered the Spiritual Realm, from that moment on he has been in the hearts and souls of all people. It was the beginning of Satya Yuga and ending of Kali Yuga (an Age we are still going through presently). So, yes, his passing is tied into "ages," calendars, similar to the Mayan calendars of ages. Maitreya was, and is, here not to destroy other faiths, but to restore the truth to all religions.

I wasted too much time with this miraculous opportunity to help others and to help change the world. My message to you is simple.

Don't do what I did. Don't waste your time. Use this opportunity, *your opportunity*, to help others attain God-Realization and change this world we live in. The time is much too short to waste.

Who Is Maitreya The Friend of All Souls?

Maitreya was born John Lee Douglas in Des Moines, Iowa in the year 1943. According to everyone who knew him, he had a tendency right from the beginning to sacrifice himself for those around him. When he was eight years old, John and his brother were playing at the top of the stairs while their father worked in the basement below. When John's brother, Dave, snuck up behind him and grabbed his waist as a joke, they both fell. Realizing they were plummeting towards disaster, John grabbed his brother and used himself as a pillow to cushion his brother's fall.

He had seconds to react, and whereas most of us would have barely even realized that we were falling, this boy, this young child, this wonderful human, immediately snapped into gear and decided to use his own body to shelter his brother's fall. This is the kind of person John was and this is the event that began his journey.

When John and Dave crashed down to the ground, John was knocked unconscious. While he was passed out, momentarily dead, John was taken into what he always referred to as Perfect Union with God. He was whole. He was Enlightened. He reached a precious state that only incredibly few in the past had even scratched the surface of. He would one day bring that opportunity to all Souls—more on that later.

John woke up moments later in worldly time, but he never fully forgot what he saw. August 7, 1951, was the day he started his journey, and the day he became Maitreya. But, when he woke up, John realized he only vaguely remembered his time in Perfect Union. It was enough to pique his interest and get the ball rolling, but the details were spotty. He couldn't remember what he'd seen or heard. He could barely recall the full Self-Realization he'd experienced through God's Grace.

Maitreya later spoke on how he believes God gave the Call in 1951 because it was shortly after mankind invented nuclear weapons and we could now destroy the entire world. He is here to champion the survival of humanity. Other religions also predicted the coming of Maitreya—to be many years in the future. But here he was, in our lifetime, and only about a thousand people knew. And now, the continued survival of humanity may be at risk.

Maitreya would spend the rest of his childhood and early adulthood trying to learn more about what had happened. It wasn't until more than 25 years later, in 1977 through tireless spiritual work, that Maitreya would finally achieve Perfect Union again, in Spirit—through his own Works. He made Two Self-Sacrifices—one by Grace, and one by Works—for the sake of all others—for your sake, for my sake. These were not just "near-death" experiences, he completely died to this world, twice. He sacrificed his Perfect Final Union with God, twice.

~⊃

CHAPTER TWO

A Lost Childhood

Life Before

It is important to share my family history. Knowing that, I believe, will help get a sense of how my troublesome personality developed. There's a line I heard somewhere, "Some people are raised. Some are forged." Maitreya completed my forging through spiritual fire.

However, please grasp this fully: this is not to say that a mostly bad childhood is what *led* me to this spiritual path. In fact, the mostly bad childhood is what *impeded* not only my own spiritual growth but in some respects the growth of the Spiritual Community.

Importantly, these two "families" are not either/or. They have always been "both/and." If I had not had the childhood I had, perhaps I would never have found Maitreya. If I had not suffered, I may not have been able to help other suffering souls. But, in a sense although not completely, the Friends' Community was my first real, true home.

I was born the eighth of nine children. We were all about two years apart. I was also born into a world of stress. Throughout her pregnancy with me, my mother was anxious. I believe her mom—my grandmother—passed away shortly before I was born. I don't know if it was my mom's stress hormones while she was carrying me that caused the anxiety I feel as an adult, but I wouldn't rule it out.

I am told that the night I was born, my dad dropped my mom off at the hospital before going right back home to finish his dinner.

By the time I came around, my parents had stopped taking pictures. Most of the baby photos in my childhood home were of my oldest sibling. By the time I showed up, there were only a few scattered occasions when my parents would believe a picture was warranted. Because of this, there are sparse remnants of evidence that my childhood ever even happened. Apparently, I also had a history of almost ruining family photos. My Dad ran for mayor of a small town in New Jersey in the mid-1960s. I was a pretty goofy kid, sometimes sticking my tongue out for the few pictures I got a chance to be in, and my mom was angry for years that I was moving around in the campaign photo. Maybe that's why they rarely took pictures of me in general. On the flip side, it may also be why I loved photography all my life. I felt moments should be captured and the camera was giving me power to have control over that.

But let me get back to the crux. It's hard to describe my memories of my mother. I recall a lot of fear, mixed with sadness; a mixture of emotions that still wells up in me when I remember her. When she passed away, I felt a peace, because she was no longer in this world—a relief difficult to describe with words. It wasn't just the hope that she herself might finally gain peace, it was that she was no longer around. She was no longer a threat to me. I literally felt a great physical relief when she was no longer in the world. I remember telling my friend Michelle *"I'm relieved"* and she asked, *"You mean that she's no longer suffering?"* and I responded, *"Not just that, it's like an unconscious fear I didn't fully know I had, is lifted off me. Like when an attacker is gone from your life."* I did not go to her funeral but, you may be surprised this was not out of spite. I donated the cost of my airfare to my sister who was burdened with a bill for the assisted living center. Mom had unfortunately outlived Dad's pension. Mom and I did have a closer relationship and connection towards the end, but the inherent childhood traumas you pile up, stay with you a long time.

I feared how violent my mom was when I was a kid. One vivid horrendous memory: I am standing in the hallway upstairs. I am compelled to glance into a bedroom—and see my mom with her hands around my younger brother's neck. He sits quietly with big eyes looking up at her. She doesn't know I can see. I am frozen. I am scared. *Is she going to choke my brother to death in front of my eyes?* She even has an unflinching, unforgiving look on her face. Her hands tightened around his neck. I don't remember anything after that.

Flash forward years later. I am visiting my parents and the story about a mother who drowned her children comes on the news. The commentators are wondering how a mother could do such a thing. Suddenly I hear my mom clearly say softly under her breath, *"Oh, I understand how."* A chill went through me but I almost laughed in amazement. I also knew this was a general sentiment she had; I at least knew she was not directing it toward any of us specifically, at that moment.

I managed to block the memory for years, until a few years ago when I was talking to my younger brother and he brought it up. *"Hey, remember when mom tried to kill me?"* He just laughed it off, though. *"Good times. No, I wouldn't have any problems after that, not at all."* But I could feel a little shock running through me. I remembered that I was there that day. That it was real. Another realization: I had been vaguely subconsciously afraid for years, that I had been the one with my hands around his neck, which made no sense, did it? We were both so young—maybe he was five and I was seven. At least that illogical fear was finally put to rest.

My heart will always break for this brother because he and his wife lost their only son to suicide. Their son was just seventeen when he laid down on the railroad tracks. It was April Fool's Day and some friends who thought it must be a joke quickly found out it was anything but. There is no coming back from that. I am proud of them both for somehow moving forward and living "with" it, since they will never get "over" this.

One of my nephews also lost his step-son to suicide just about three years later, also at seventeen years old, this time by a self-inflicted gunshot.

Too much for one family, isn't it? But this world involves so much suffering until we transcend it.

My heart will always be heavy that I did not save either of these two young, impulsive boys who had not fulfilled the gift of a full life. I did help them with spiritual communion after they were gone. I guided them to God and Maitreya as best I could—to accept responsibility for what was done and to move on through the consequences and on to a better life in spirit. The first nephew took a long time to pass over—partly because he felt he needed to stay near his parents who were so distraught. They are all finally healing now. I actually saw the spirit of this nephew one day. This was out of the left corner of my eye, while awake and sitting in my apartment. I saw him walking by in jeans and a red t-shirt. I felt it was his way of saying he was okay now.

The memory of my mom strangling this brother would creep into consciousness every once in a while, but I would push it back to its recesses. But to jump ahead a bit, it may be part of what led me to be in an abusive relationship with a crazy man who literally strangled me. Was I trying to recreate that childhood memory in some way? It was sometime in the mid 1990's. I sat on my bed while the crazy new "boyfriend" put his hands around my neck and kept squeezing. His eyes turned black. I didn't fight at first, I just sat there resigned, *"This is it. I'm going to die."* But something made him stop. Not me, because I just sat there. But he stopped trying to kill me. At that point I jumped into action and ran to the kitchen and waved a knife around while repeatedly yelling, *"Get out!"* He finally left but I later discovered that he didn't go right home. He immediately went to the police station nearby. He made a preemptive report that I had waved a knife at him and threatened him out of nowhere. I found this out, when I arrived at the same station to make my own report—a few days later. Can you believe this man? I was wearing a turtleneck or crew neck sweater to hide marks still visible on my neck. I decided that at least an "incident report" would be proactive without an actual legal battle. The young cop looked steadily at me after I told him what happened, and with some compassion in his voice said, "*he already filed a report against you. It's just your word against his.*" I gave up. At first it bothered me that no one believed me—bothered me a lot—but eventually I learned to accept responsibility for putting myself in that position in the first place. I knew something was off about the guy and I took wrong actions, anyway, because I wanted a relationship. I foolishly thought it was a plus that he knew Maitreya, but I didn't know he was full-on crazy.

Rationalizing wrong or bad relationships was my pattern for several years. Another boyfriend (years after the strangling one), slapped me hard across the face. (It contributed to TMJ problems). Did I immediately end it with him? No, I kept going back, because I felt I needed to be in a relationship. I did at least end up legally assisting his children in a custody battle (I believe that part was truly "meant to be.") I was now in my 40's and didn't want to be alone.

For several dysfunctional relationships, I'm sure the cliché on some level was a certainty: "That's what love is, someone hitting me," played a major part in my gravitating toward more abusive relationships.

But truly, the fear of a mother seems so contrary to how childhood is meant to be. It was not only that younger brother who received the blunt force of my mom's anger. She hit all of us, and hit me quite often. She would continue to beat me as I was balled up on the ground. I also remember hiding under the stairs muttering "*I hate Mommy, I hate Mommy, I hate Mommy…*" just low enough that nobody would hear it. I even rocked myself to sleep at night, back and forth, repeating that same mantra over and over, "*I hate Mommy, I hate Mommy,*" as I tried to self-soothe while rocking myself. The strange thing is that recently one of my middle sisters told me she would do the same thing—rock herself at night and repeat over and over the same dysfunctional mantra, "I hate Mommy." I don't know if I saw and heard her and copied her behavior, or if we just happened to do the same thing. We joked that it could have been a horror movie with nine kids all rocking, tossing themselves back and forth and chanting, "*I hate Mommy,*" throughout the house. When you grow up in a house like that, you may eventually escape, but a part of you never really gets out.

My other comfort was hiding under the stairs. When opening the front door of the house, the stairs were immediately to the right. There was a perfect cubby hole under that staircase. An ideal hiding place for a solitary young soul such as myself. I hid not only my body but my mind and spirit as I secretly closed the little door while no one was watching. I sat on boxes and clutter in absolute peace; hiding, protecting, insulating, enveloping myself in my own made-up security. There were old photos and cameras in there and a leather smell from the camera cases that I treasured. Boredom or hunger would eventually drive me out. I have no memory of anyone ever noticing me going in or out of that hiding spot. It was mine for years until I was physically too cumbersome, even though I mentally still yearned for my own special place.

Perhaps hiding under the stairs also contributed to my photography interests. My Dad had stored old cameras there and I would examine them and imagine using them. I not only hid my body under the stairs, but I also hid within my mind. I sometimes would escape to another life through books, huddled under blankets with a flashlight, reading books beyond my years, some taken from my siblings' school assignments. Somehow reading also became analogous to my future—I sensed that my own life would not remain dismal— there would be different chapters, and the ending was up to my own actions, in a still unknown way. I just had to wait for more chapters.

I am sure abusive incidents with my mother are the reason I had all these anger issues as an adult. Her and my father—yes, he hit me too, but not nearly as much as my mom. Once when I was a teenager we were in the driveway and my dad slapped me because I talked back to him. For the life of me I cannot remember what we were fighting about, but I remember looking at him in anger for backhanding me, and his cold reaction. *"Take that look off your face or I'll take it off,"* before smacking me hard across the face, again. I remember silently retorting, *"Well, of course that 'look' is on my face—you just slapped it."* I often wondered where logic had gone. Our childless neighbors saw the whole thing. Over the years, we would joke around, *"That's why they stayed childless."*

Being the eighth of nine children, I often struggled to be and feel "heard," especially through countless discussions at the dinner table. I followed in my mind, but could not articulate much; or if I managed to attempt to join in, I felt ignored. Time passed and my body got bigger but these ideas did not always grow up. The belief that I will not be heard lingers to this day. Sadly, this affects my speech and conversational patterns: I repeat concepts a lot. I will repeat myself until either we all give up—or the relief of an acknowledgment that I am truly heard is given to me. You can see it is a condition from this background of never really feeling heard. I developed a tendency to over-explain, repeat myself, and interrupt others. When I feel I am truly heard, all of those habits relax and dissipate.

A major trauma affected us all. When I was fourteen, my 18-year-old sister Mary Jo was killed in a car accident. Of course, this impacted each member of the family in separate ways. It was a strange moment of togetherness on a summer day when we gathered around the "war table,"—the kitchen table—while my dad and older sisters and brothers strategize how best to get my *other* sister notified and back home from the same rock concert at Watkins Glen, New York. The same concert that Mary Jo was on her way to when her boyfriend's van tipped over in the rain and she died. My other sister mentioned once that she thinks she met a lot of famous people backstage that day, but she does not remember.

All the initial shock and energy went into finding the other sister and getting her home. They somehow did it, back before computers. I am not certain but I believe or heard that Mary Jo's boyfriend later became a priest, presumably due to guilt which is unfortunate. This sister had premonitions before the accident. We (three of the sisters) all slept in the same room at that time, and one night Mary Jo had a nightmare. She woke up afraid, saying she dreamed she was being crushed. This was only a couple of weeks before her accident. I don't like to focus on that part, as I know she eventually found her beautifully deserved peace.

Mary Jo and I were not particularly close. I was not truly close with any of my siblings. Our childhood home was an "every person for themselves" atmosphere, at least from my point of view. (I have since read that this is common behavior in an abusive environment). I do not fault my siblings one bit. They were all dealing with their own traumas, barely healing themselves, never mind being able to try to heal each other. This atmosphere was combined with being one of the youngest and not "in with the in-crowd." I was more introverted and not interested in drugs and drinking, so that pretty much sealed the deal and made me more of an outsider. I recall being surprised hearing certain expressions in the 60's and 70's, like people "soul-searching" or "finding oneself." I wondered, why anyone would search for something they already were, although I did not quite understand my own meanderings sometimes. I tried to be more extroverted as a young adult but it never felt authentic.

Bear with me, but another painful memory occurred soon after the loss of Mary Jo. I heard my mom crying in their bedroom on a Saturday afternoon. I gathered my courage, opened the door, and hugged her. This was extremely rare for us to do anything remotely like this. *Are we actually hugging?* She cried a bit and then she thanked me. Then, completely out of nowhere, went on to tell me that she never wanted me. She was not sure about all her nine pregnancies. Ten, if you count the miscarriage she had when she was young. It was part of being Catholic and part of the time she lived in. But, as I remember, she said, "*I especially did not want you. I was pregnant with you when my own mother had recently died, and I was filled with grief and did not want to go through another birth.*" She looked me in the eyes, as if she was telling me something wonderfully helpful.

Seemingly unconcerned, or unconscious of the fact, that she was possibly destroying what sliver of a relationship we had. "*I just didn't want you.*" She mentioned something about one of my brothers too, as not being the timing, she would have wanted. "*But especially you.*" I sarcastically commented to myself inwardly, "*Well, at least I'm special.*"

I reflect later, at least she said it *calmly*, unlike the rants she would go into while hitting and striking me over and over and repeating endlessly "*I wish you were never born.*" Again, it is hard to describe the beatings. I would first be standing as she would slap me hard on the face, and then I am eventually balled up on the floor trying to protect myself while she keeps backhanding me over and over on any area she could reach, all while being as verbally abusive as she could muster. She never quietly hit us. She always said terribly ugly things when doing so. She would say things like, "*I wish I never had you kids. I wish you were never born. I'll give you something to cry about. Who do you think you are?*" That's about all I can remember, but the, "*I wish you were never born*" seemed to be her favorite go-to phrase.

Other than beatings and emotional scars, she did manage to give me a physical scar under my right eye that I still notice to this day (although it's now blending with wrinkles). She was slapping me and her fingernail cut down my eyelid and lower eye area. I defiantly made a point of mentioning it at dinner, "*Look at my red eye, and the scratch under it, Mom did that!*" Yet no one said a word.

My brother Harry, who is two years older than me, currently does not remember the beatings. This is astonishing news to me. It had never occurred to me during the times he defended our mother in later years, that he really didn't remember anything. The odd thing was, I had witnessed some of it. When we were around nine and eleven, he was being mean to the neighborhood kids. He came in the front door and she grabbed him, yelling and smacking him, saying "*You're a bully,*" over and over. I sat and watched from the stairs, realizing, "*Wait, aren't you being a bully to him? And he's only a kid,*" until I think I told her to stop. I'm not sure if I dared to tell her, or if I only said that in my head.

In our younger days, we would often go on errands with my mom. One time she was yelling at some of us in the A&P grocery store. A man came up and asked her to stop, and she was furious after that. When we got in the car, she proceeded to slap us all. I was in the back of the car. I remember her reaching back. She said we had humiliated her. I remember pleading with her to stop, but it took her a while to come down off her rage. We can conclude this is a type of "rage-aholic" situation, no?

My sisters later filled me in on incidents that happened long before I was born. Our mom expected my sister to come home early from school because of an appointment, but she got caught up in an art class. She was taking art lessons from a woman who lived nearby. She was thrilled with her picture of the Easter Bunny and its cute cotton balls placed just so, and went skipping down the street and burst in the door to proudly show mom her beautiful project. Mom proceeded to scream and hit her because they were late. She ripped the picture up and threw it away. She then pushed Annie's head into the sink to pour water on her face, to get her to stop crying, which also ended up causing her to have a bloody nose.

This was when they were temporarily living in a tiny place, while the house which was to become the family home was being built. They were late to visit Dad at the new property.

It was also around that time, years before I was born, that one of my brothers went with a neighborhood kid down to a lake, and the other boy drowned. They were only maybe four years old and no one is sure why on earth they went off unsupervised. I feel terrible for my brother that he has had to hold on to all that trauma, along with everything else we went through as kids, all from such a young age.

I was told of an incident when the oldest sister Elaine, at around 16, came home from a high school dance with her hair teased up in a beehive, which was the style at the time. My mom was furious and grabbed her hair, pulled her into the bathroom and shoved her head under the water in the sink while screaming obscenities. I believe the word "whore" was used.

Apparently, there was yet another (much earlier) time when this oldest sister was supposed to be watching her younger sister and wasn't, so Mom hit Elaine over the head with a heavy iron pan. Both Elaine and Annie were quite young, in early grade school, really too young to be watching each other anyway. The injury caught some attention at school—they set up a home visit from social workers. This was *extremely* unusual in the 1950's and 60's. I am fairly certain it just infuriated my mom further and caused a few more beatings, after the home visit ended.

My sister mentioned another memory in which they were all at the small house. My sister was in around third grade and brother Mike was in maybe the second grade. My brother thought it would be a cool idea for him and another kid to break into an old, abandoned house nearby. Annie stayed on the porch and did not go in, but the police were called. It was the first time my sister saw our Dad beat our brother so badly it frightened her.

So, when Dad turned and asked Anne if she had broken into the abandoned house too, she of course said, "*Oh no, I wasn't there.*" But her conscience bothered her. In the middle of the night, she went to mom and poked her awake and whispered, "*I was there.*" Mom never said anything. Either she later forgot because she had been sleeping, or she felt enough beatings had taken place to her satisfaction. Who knows?

I remember mom saying when we were older "*You were all sweet babies, I liked when you were babies.*" Whether this is true or not, several incidents happened where my mom hit us as babies as well. Anne recalls when she caught Mom slapping the youngest who was just an infant, so Anne grabbed him and ran upstairs and hid in a room until Dad came home. Then she just quietly walked down and put him in the crib and nobody said anything about it.

I do believe my older brothers and sisters did the best they could, especially the sisters, and that no one in any way should place blame on themselves. No child should need to take care of another child—particularly when they themselves are *also* not being cared for.

One of my very first memories was being in a crib, and crying for a long time—filled with a dread that no one was coming. I remember a feeling of fear. Even though I was a baby, my memories are mostly of emotions that no one is there and I am afraid. I think I remember her being rough with me then, even though I was less than two years old. That was my earliest memory. How a baby would know dread, I can't say, but that was my first feeling-memory.

Another early—quite clear—memory is starting kindergarten and being overjoyed that I would be out of the house. I was mean to my mother and angrily mumbled at her, "*I'm glad I'll be away from you.*" This sweet-looking kid sneering at her!

And I was told by my sisters (when I later wondered if I had done something wrong to cause our mom to react over the years), that I was in fact a sweet quiet kid. I remember most of us were fairly well behaved and not predisposed (or allowed) to indulge in tantrums of any kind.

In looking back at this young age, I also have a distinct memory of having full thoughts in my preschool mind, fully formed in spirit, and yet at that time, I did not have the language skills at such a young age to articulate them out loud. I have heard this is a common recollection from those who discuss reincarnation. It is the feeling of "*how do I get these thoughts out of my head and communicate—when I don't know the language yet?*"

As much as I was happy for my great escape, I would shortly come to learn that life was not much better at Our Lady of The Valley school from first through eighth grade. The Catholic nuns were still permitted to use corporal punishment in the 1970's, and I had several altercations. Most of the aggressive nuns liked to routinely pull my long hair, usually sneaking up on me from behind while I was at my desk. They would also regularly hit my knuckles with a ruler. The infractions were perhaps talking or passing notes, since I was usually a good student. As puberty arrived, I became more angry and less likely to take the austere nuns' shenanigans. I ruminated on how a Sister (nun) in school could be such a bully, but a sister at home could be so sweet.

It was fifth or sixth grade when Sister Ann called me out to the hallway, suddenly poking and shoving me in the chest, her robes swishing around her as if they were angry too. She asked, "*How dare you glare at me?*" I tried to articulate that I did not feel that they were following Jesus' teachings, but I said it quite angrily. We stared at each other—a spiritual showdown, right there in the elementary school hallway. Like cowboys in a standoff, guns drawn, with a line in the sand. My message had clearly not been well received.

The school only allowed group bathroom breaks twice a day, so I became unhealthily adept at holding in my urine. Some kids weren't so adaptable to this bathroom rule, but we wouldn't tease them much if they made a mess, because we all knew it could happen to anyone at any time. We had to line up in height order. The same nun who poked me in the chest would go ballistic if anyone was talking while in line for the restrooms. She would push and shove the first kid in line, and there'd we go—all stumbling back in a tumbling domino effect.

In reflecting back, being hit was a way of life during childhood, both at home and at school. I wondered why adults were so miserable and why they had to make kids miserable too. One older sister said when she was a young kid our mom threw her on the bed and just kept hitting and slapping her over and over. Anne was determined not to cry. But determination could only go so far under the weight of a fully grown adult taking their aggression out on you, no? Finally, she just had to whimper and Mom stopped hitting. My sister said something clicked in her brain, feeling like she had finally realized exactly what she was dealing with: a mother who wants her to cry and will stop hitting if she gets what she wants.

I know the oldest also tells of a plan she once had to try to get everyone together to run away, because she felt responsible as the elder sibling. But she did not plan it well and they didn't have enough food or a strategy as to where to go. They went a few blocks away with a few sandwiches. Our sister Anne judged that and decided she was going to be a better planner one day. They both did go on to have successful careers (Elaine in producing news shows and Anne in social work and teaching—both being good at planning and directing others).

Not much relief yet, dear reader. Life in the public high school was not much better than the elementary Catholic school. It was a different kind of hell. I had the mistaken hope that teachers in a public school would be nice and kind since they were not nuns or priests. They were not. They were all quite mean and rude, even mocking me at times. I was like the girl wearing black in the movie *The Breakfast Club*—a depressed loner, an outsider.

September of my freshman year was my worst nightmare. The summer just prior to that had been miserable. Our family was dealing with the death of Mary Jo in July. And, our grandfather had died just a few months before Mary Jo. He was staying at our house and watching Watergate on TV. He stood up, yelled at Nixon, had a heart attack, and passed away. My brother Mike found him, and had to sit me down on the couch and tell me when I got home from school at the end of eighth grade. My Dad was a bit withdrawn after his father passed away but he didn't talk about it much; and then months later he had to deal with his daughter's sudden passing. I did feel for him even then. A random memory still comes and goes to this day—we went to a small house my sister had just moved to before her accident. I was instructed to take whatever I wanted as a remembrance. I felt uncomfortable, as if we were being crass to her memory. But I finally grabbed a blue old-fashioned tin container. Turned out that she had gotten that from Pops, who died shortly before she did. I still have it to this day. It is just a cheap tin, but I treasure it.

And with this background, I was thrown into a large, rowdy, noisy cauldron of sarcasm and judgment not only from other students but from those I thought would be in charge. Only one truly kind teacher stood out, the typing instructor. That's probably why I was so comfortable in offices for the rest of my working life.

Some major world events contributed to inward chaos. When I was a toddler, my family was in shock when John F. Kennedy was assassinated. I recall trying to ask what happened and felt confusion, mainly because I only had a general idea of what a president even was. I was a little older when Robert Kennedy was killed. I was already overloaded by being exposed to the nightly news of Vietnam conflicts while our family was directly affected.

My brother was in Da Nang at the time. (We wrote each other letters. I would describe childhood events like my new Stingray bike with the banana seat. He would only write about music or food or weather, and that he missed everyone. He did not give much detail of his actual war activities.) He came home around 1972. He was physically in one piece, but he suffered with PTSD the rest of his life.

I also recall my Dad waking us all up around midnight to gather around the TV set and watch man walk on the moon for the first time. Even then, my mindset was, "Why? Don't we have enough to do on this planet?"

Point being, chaos and change seemed all around and within me.

A particularly bad episode occurred toward the end of that freshman year in the late 1970's. My mother decided to take me to a psychiatrist. I had been sitting around the house practically catatonic. (I give her credit for at least wanting to do something.) So, there we sat in a shrink's office. I barely spoke to him and just wrung my hands a lot for some reason. He decided to put me on Thorazine—an incredibly potent anti-psychotic—even though I was depressed and not in psychosis. A fun side effect happened, as my eyes rolled into the back of my head one day while in class. I guess the drugs at least did help me stay quite calm about it. Another kind person shone through at that time—a young man with long hair who also liked to wear long coats, HW. (Interestingly, he looked like the character Judd Nelson played in Breakfast Club. That movie was a little too realistic for me.) He stood up, took my arm, and led me through the hallway to the nurse's office. He made sure I was okay and he told other kids not to mock me. We were good friends for several years. He even lived on the same street where my family had lived before I was born, Lewis Street, which we thought was a good sign.

In my first job at a large corporation, I worked in the mailroom for a while. One of the young men there had a lobotomy. He talked about it quite openly and so did the coworkers. It was both frightening and fascinating to talk to someone whose brain had been mutilated so that he could function in the world without anxiety. What a crazy time. I had been put on Thorazine and then shortly after, I met this lobotomized young man, and both of us were not even in our 20's yet. I guess I should be thankful I didn't have that barbaric surgery, too.

When I was a teenager, my mom suddenly acted nice to me for about a week or so. I still acted temperamental and withdrawn, but part of me did take notice and enjoy that she was being kinder. Until she said, "*Here I've been nice to you all week, and you still look at me like that.*" The sinking realization came upon me; it was all just an act. One more reason I do not always take much stock or belief in hearing the words "I love you," since part of me always questions what is real. Love became a mysterious puzzle from a young age.

You can perhaps guess the next part. I fled the family home as soon as I turned 18. I couldn't wait to be on my own.

Family and cousins photo.
I am holding my sisters' hands and looking the other way.

My Dad's campaign photo—I have my tongue out.

We re-created the campaign photo, late 1990s.
At least this time I just closed my eyes, instead of sticking my tongue out.

My Journey Begins

By age 23, I was married, and living in San Francisco with my husband at the time, and I had not yet begun my spiritual journey.

As newlyweds, the first few years with my husband were fun and exciting. Likely fueled by young hormones, I was mostly happy and content. Marriage was new to me, and it felt strange. I'd felt what I thought was love in relationships before, but not as deeply as I did with my husband. We were bonded, and that increased when I experienced a health scare.

I woke one day with pelvic pain and flushed away what I assumed was a strange blood clot. I went onward with the daily routine. While sitting in a college class, in extreme pain, I realized something was wrong but I waited until class was over until I finally went to the student medical office. The nurse wasn't sure what to make of my stoicism, but she told me to get to a hospital. She asked me if I wanted an ambulance or would I like to call someone to get a ride. We finally called my husband (no cell phones yet, but we reached him). He arrived with panic all over his face. I'll never forget the bumpy ride in his truck, gripping the door handle in pain over each impact. He seemed petrified and kept telling me how pale I was. We were in the emergency room for hours—not just because of the normal wait time, but because different doctors were trying to decide what to do. One mentioned that I was too calm for it to be what they thought it might be. They surmised I did not appear to be in quite enough pain. They didn't want me to undergo unnecessary surgery. Finally, when one doctor saw me shivering and asked me if I was cold, I said no. I was scared and the pain had been going on for hours. The decision was finally made: it must be an ectopic pregnancy, and surgery was in order. Years later I realized that the physical shock made me revert to childhood coping mechanisms: *Act like you are OK. Act like you are fine. Don't let on as to what's really happening. Don't think about this right now. Think about it later.* My stoicism and reserved manner were almost the cause of my death, at only 24 years of age.

We had gotten pregnant, but it was into an ectopic pregnancy, and I became gravely ill when my tube burst. It was a scary and painful experience, but it ultimately brought the two of us closer—at least for a while.

My husband and I were so thankful and happy that I recovered that we didn't talk much about the possibility that I would never have children. But there's more to marriage than feeling happy. Despite being married, and having my family, I never really felt fully loved.

I always felt like I was on the outside looking in, wanting more. I was happy when I married my husband and we had a strong connection, but there was always something a bit off. Something was missing—in me, not necessarily in him. I'd look up at birds flying in a V formation and think to myself, *"See that last one at the end? The one barely keeping up. That's me."* Most likely because of my life growing up. My mother and I had an incredibly tough relationship. Nevertheless, I resigned myself to living my life as is. I had a husband, some friends, so what if I never felt fully loved?

With such a lax attitude, it didn't take long for things to change in our marriage once our lifestyle differences started to become more known. He was a partying musician, and I was trying to build up a more serious life for myself. I wanted to settle down and I felt he wanted to keep living like he was in his early 20s. Our growing apart didn't happen overnight, it was more of a slow burn, smoldering underneath until we were finally, and officially, growing apart.

A long painful phone call took place after I moved to L.A. I still see myself huddled in a local supermarket phone booth in 1985 or so, clutching the corded phone, checking in on him and us. I caused him pain by leaving on that bus, but I needed to do it; although, a part of me was still wondering if he would also move from San Francisco to Los Angeles and join me. To his credit, he did visit later, and even stayed at our Holy Ashram. He was polite to Maitreya who, of course, had an impact on him Spiritually. It was partly because of his Contact with Maitreya that his visit went so well. We were then at least able to have a civil uncomplicated divorce as we slowly accepted that we had to move on.

Maybe that's why I was so open and accepting of what happened after my marriage. Or, perhaps it was just fate, Divine Intervention. That is what I know in my heart to be true. It was Destiny.

In 1983, seven years after Maitreya's second Self-Realization and Self Sacrifice, my new life began. A friend of mine sent me a letter out of the blue. Shanti and I went to high school together in New Jersey. She's a tiny, but intense Armenian woman with curly hair, piercing eyes, and a beautiful smile that she doesn't use nearly enough. We had a few classes together, but I wouldn't say that we were good friends back in high school. She was more popular than I was and—much more of a rebel, a cool girl. I, on the other hand, was a complete outcast.

But in the first year after we graduated high school, Shanti and I happened to get jobs together at the same bank as clerical assistants. Coincidence or fate, that's up for debate, but it was then that we became friends—I definitely say Fate. We were fast friends before she moved out of New Jersey. When she moved to California ahead of me, I set her up with my brother and sister-in-law in San Francisco. I had no idea at the time just how significant this move would be, and how much it would set the stage to completely change both of our lives.

I followed Shanti out to San Francisco about a year later and we became roommates. Eventually I moved out, to live with the man who would become my husband. Shanti eventually moved south, miles away, to Redondo Beach. And it was while she was living there that I got her letter. She mentioned that she was renting a room from a Guru she'd met in Redondo Beach. I wondered if she was in a cult. I was so worried that I told my husband I'd be back in a few days, packed up some of my belongings in San Francisco and headed out to visit Shanti. I was ready to drag her back home with me if I had to.

But when I got there, I was immediately awestruck. This wasn't at all what I had expected. Shanti wasn't in trouble at all, and she certainly wasn't in a cult. She introduced me to her Guru, also known as a Satguru. I remember the indescribable sense of joy I felt when I first set eyes on him.

The instant I met Maitreya, I knew in my deepest heart he was real and true and special to the world. Maitreya's gentle face had long, flowing reddish blonde hair and a full beard framing it. His eyes were a deep hazel. He wore a paisley shirt and blue jeans. He was thin. He greeted me warmly by holding on to both of my hands. He offered me aloe vera from a plant to put on a burn near my mouth. (From that time on, I have had aloe vera plants in my home.) Meeting him was breathtaking. It filled me with a joy that I feared might only be fleeting; it wound up being anything but. When I first saw him, I was transported out of this material realm and into the spiritual one. I felt divine peace and bliss. It felt, and this is in no way an exaggeration, like meeting Jesus in real life for the first time. I felt all of this and yet, we had barely spoken a few words to each other. So much for brainwashing with words. And yet this was one of the most defining moments of my entire life.

That was when I knew this spiritual teacher was for real. I knew I had to know more and become involved. I knew right then that this was what I had been missing. All that time I'd spent on the outside looking in, never feeling totally loved or totally connected to the people in my life, that was all over now. I went back to San Francisco State to finish college (I was a commuter student, also working part-time), and to see if my husband would move with me to L.A.

Before you jump the gun, and judge me as I first judged Shanti, let me assure you, this isn't a cult. In fact, Maitreya later gave talks and seminars in the area at libraries and parks, on how to recognize a true cult and their characteristics. The main thing Maitreya made clear was how cults took away a person's freedom and dealt in censorship and brainwashing. Maitreya always prioritized our own personal freedom, personal choice, and the undeniable personal responsibility that goes with those things. In a nutshell, cults are easy to get into, and hard to get out of. In our Spiritual Community, everyone is welcome, and everyone is welcome to leave.

I had another memorable "phone booth" call. I can see myself sitting in an actual wooden mahogany booth in the college library hallway, dialing the number on the literature Shanti had given me. I talked with Maitreya himself on the phone, taking time out of his day to speak to me. I was filled with hope for a new future. He told me to consider my choices carefully and follow my heart. Just hearing his voice on the phone changed me in ways that only those who also experienced what we called The Changes with Maitreya would truly understand.

Whatever happened, whatever was waiting for me, no matter how drastically I would have to adjust my life or even my marriage, I knew at that moment that the only thing left was to make it official.

Married! 1982

CHAPTER THREE

My Holy Initiation
and Spiritual Experiences

Holy Initiation

It didn't take me long to receive Maitreya's Holy Initiation. I didn't receive Holy Initiation directly from Maitreya himself; it was transmitted to me by Shanti. That's the beauty of it—that any Maitreyian in Good Faith may transmit Maitreya's Holy Initiation and Universal God's Supreme Promise.

Even though Maitreya was not in front of me physically, the moment I received it, I knew a bond had been formed with him that would never break. I immediately sensed that I was more than just a personality, a mind, a body. I knew my True Self as a Pure Spirit. I may be limited in body, but I am truly unlimited in Spirit. I felt Divine Bliss for an instant, as I experienced everything melt-away, and expand outwards into all Eternity.

As Maitreya explained, it's like a lamp that's sitting there but not plugged in. It's functional. Everything the lamp needs to one day be, everything it has the potential to become, is already there. The True Enlightenment I received from my Holy Initiation was like being plugged in for the first time. I was forever changed. I—and "I" was both gone, transcended and still there— immediately noticed the world was different, as I was connected to ALL and all at once. One of our core principles is to, "*See God in All and All in God,*" and that was truly one of my first real experiential lessons. My life was forever changed. This was the first of many direct experiences of knowing my True Self as One with Universal Spirit.

As with most spiritual experiences, it's hard to exactly encapsulate with words. I immediately felt the walls within me crash down the second I accepted Holy Initiation. I opened up beyond the borders of what my past self was. I felt a connectedness, a oneness with all. And the connected-ness didn't even stop with humans. I even felt an affinity with animals after my Holy Initiation. I'd always seen animals as separate from us. I always kind of assumed they didn't really have souls. But, after Shanti transmitted Holy Initiation onto me, any time I looked at any other living thing in the eyes—animal or human—I felt their True Self as Spirit which is One with Universal Spirit. This was my first spiritual experience and the most profound because it was the first day of my unending Spiritual Bond with The Friend. I learned what an honor it is to truly follow a great spiritual master.

Some might wonder, "Couldn't you just go to the Universal God directly without a middleman—or woman?" Sure. Some people attain Oneness with Universal God all on their own. But why not have a Guide? Is there anything wrong with having a guide when you climb a mountain? Is there something wrong with having tour guides when you travel? Is there anything wrong with having mentors in the physical realm? Why not receive spiritual guidance from The Friend of All Souls, one who has been up the mountain before and now is truly residing within the Spiritual Realm, available to all who may call on him.

Yes, dear readers, he was a man. Too many times, I feel intense divisiveness from women who may be on a spiritual path but object to having a male as a Guide. I often find women parroting the phrase, "I hate men." And I want to ask, "Do you? Or do you hate only the men who have wronged you?" Some women who fight for equality are often the ones who actually just want a change in regime. So it is important, before a judgment is passed, to realize that gender is not a truth bearer but merely a fact. Had he been a woman, would you then decide to perhaps find out for yourself? Touchy issue these days. But I am puzzled why anyone who professes to believe in unity and oneness of Spirit, will also espouse general anti-man sentiments. But we all have our own struggles and journeys.

Speaking of struggles, as it turned out, I was to become the example of how "not to be." My name does mean Faith Through Experience—not just Blind Faith. I needed to learn what it truly meant to be both a follower and a leader and how neither can be without the other. Learning to care more about our Holy Cause than being "accepted" by non-initiates and unenlightened souls was a crucial lesson.

I quickly learned that "following" meant opening my mind up to Higher Truths, experiencing those truths myself, using my own God-Given Intelligence on the Truths bequeathed to me, and being willing to change my small ego-self around such Truth. This is as opposed to demanding that Truth "change" itself, to fit my small self (which, of course, then becomes a lie).

On the foundation of our religion, people live different kinds of lives—there are no social rules such as vegetarianism or not, married or not, money or simpleness. Each Maitreyian could live very different lives and yet each have at their core the same bond of following Maitreya home to Universal God and giving that gift to others, as our unifying adhesive for eternity.

On a material note, Maitreya had asked if I minded receiving Holy Initiation on the 13th of the month (July). I said no, I don't want to be superstitious. Sometimes I wonder if there's something to that whole 13 thing. I wonder if I had waited past that one day, could that have made a difference in what was to follow? (Kidding, sort of). It still surprises me when I am in a building that does not have a 13th floor. How did we, as a society, decide to be superstitious in this day and age about a number, even in the engineering of buildings? But maybe there is something to it. I sometimes look at 13 as my lucky number since it is my spiritual birthday of receiving the most meaningful gift possible—God's Promise through Maitreya the Friend, although I may have caused bad luck to the Community.

Changes Over the Years

I was immediately changed from the moment of accepting Maitreya's Holy Initiation. But, the more gradual changes within me happened over many years. Each Community member could always see the changes in each other, much easier than seeing the changes in ourselves. I saw Shanti change from sometimes being fearful and reserved, to being bold, courageous, forthright, and fearless in the face of any enemy. I witnessed Tara changing from being self-conscious, to caring more about others and their spiritual development and using her voice to help others. I observed Ila changing from being a bit meek, to being vocal and strong in her faith, no matter what the circumstances.

The changes are like a microwave—slowly, and from the inside, out. I changed from extreme defensiveness to slowly becoming more aware of other people's realities. I see now, how too self-involved I can be. My personality changed from extreme judgmentalism to more tolerant. (However, I also learned what should, and should not be, tolerated.) I changed from acting like I knew everything, to constantly learning and being surprised about how much I don't know. *How does one know what it is that they don't know yet?* After constant spiritual enlightenments, I became humbler, much less strident. And yet, I am in awe of the greatness of the Universal Spirit within me and within all of Life. I embraced the principle of truly changing myself around universal truths, instead of expecting truth to conform around my small self.

Before my spiritual progression, my mind was strict and rigid. I had specific requirements as to what people should or shouldn't do. People were never quite reaching my imagined standards. As Maitreya would say, "*Turn that finger around, and point it toward yourself.*"

Always good advice. It took me years to realize what a boring world it would be if everyone only did what *I* thought they should.

In time, I transform from just living as a body, to knowing that my True Self is the Spirit, using the body as a vehicle. I transform from acting in a knee-jerk manner often out of ego, to being self-aware of my actions and their true source. I transform from interpreting life through an intellect in the mental realm, to transcending the material realm and living momentarily in the Spiritual Realm. I learn the difference between "mind full," and real "mindfulness." I also learn, slowly through the years, the true inescapable principle of self-responsibility.

As The Friend said, *"Let it be known, that each and every man who reads or speaks my words bears full responsibility for the meanings he puts upon them that are not my own. And let those who truly hunger and thirst after The Truth, the Whole Truth and Nothing but The Truth, seek the righteous meaning of my words, not through his own prejudice or that of another, but through God's Divine Grace within the Secret Inner Sanctuary of his Heart. For whosoever shall seek The Truth, without prejudice or preconception, unto him it shall be revealed."* (The Friend, 6/11/2001.) This new spiritual worldview was a spark, that grew to a flame, that grew to an ever-present fire, all within the Secret Inner Sanctuary of my Heart, from that moment of receiving Holy Initiation to this day.

After Shanti transmitted The Friend's and Universal God's Holy Initiation, I went back to San Francisco and back to my husband. I stayed for another year. I will always remember the first time, after returning, following the steps of meditation which we call Inner Divine Communion. The very first time I called on The Friend to be active in spirit within the Secret Inner Sanctuary of my heart, I was a bit skeptical. I wondered, *"Is this just a mental imagination or leap of faith?"* However, as The Friend always said, this is a Way of Direct Experience, not just Blind Faith. This also happens to be the definition of my name: Shraddha, Faith Through Experience.

As I sat cross-legged on my bed in my San Francisco apartment, I called on The Friend and, wham, I felt His Presence! I felt him in my heart, mind, and Spirit! He was there with me! I was filled with an indescribable Universal Peace and Love. I realized, this is just the beginning of a beautiful spiritual journey to find my True Self. From that time onward, and thousands of times by now, whenever I call upon The Friend, there is complete faith that he is truly with me and I never walk alone.

Over the years, numerous spiritual experiences occurred during Inner Divine Communion where I experienced Oneness with Universal God. These experiences are not just intellectual. While intellect and belief are a fine starting place, I experience the transcendence from this material world, to dwell in the spiritual realm as my true self. I am immersed in the ocean like a drop of water returning to the sea. The first moment was true Bliss, in a place I never before knew existed. Just moments, many moments over the years, and then returning to this world to continue my spiritual practices and lessons. With remembrances, that my True Self is Spirit, which is truly One with Universal Spirit.

I learned from Maitreya that Inner Divine Communion, and all true meditation, is not the stopping or cessation of thoughts. It is the practice of *observing* the thoughts—and letting them go, over and over, as if sitting on a bus bench watching the cars go by. We witness each sensation and thought and let them go. In time, I realize, *Oh, I am the Observer! I am the one Witnessing the mind's thoughts. I am not my mind. I am not my body or brain or personality. I am True Spirit. That same Spirit that is One within all and All within One.* This is one of Maitreya The Friend's many gifts.

Chanting our Holy Dharma Mantra "*Jai Bhagavan Ji,*" (pronounced Jay-Bhag-Wan-Gee, which means Victory to Universal God), I am transported to my true nature and self as One with God. As the chanting gets softer and subsides and then is just inward and no longer outward, I am truly aware within the depths of Spirit—who I really am. I AM THAT, I AM.

At one point Maitreya recommends looking at a clock. "*Watch the hands of the clock. See only that. See how long you can go without thoughts interfering. When they interfere, start over. Be in that Moment. Know who you really are.*" I never got many minutes in, but I still do that practice occasionally to center myself, to get out of the purely material world. (Sometimes I wonder if kids will even know what hands on a clock are, since it's pre-digital.)

Maitreya mentioned how this mindfulness is reminiscent of Buddhism. As Buddha determined, it was no point in teaching people about God when they couldn't even control or watch their own minds. I found it fascinating that Buddhism predicted another Maitreya. But I was not able to reach any or awaken them that the day had come. Similar to Hinduism and other religions; they are adamant about it occurring in a certain timeframe or year in the future. Perhaps some will realize some day that Universal God ordained that Maitreya needed to appear in our time—and changed God's timeline because of mankind's destructive choices. But here I go again, reflecting on possibilities that may have been or might still be.

The Early Days

There were a lot of firsts when I first arrived at the Ashram—our former spiritual communal center. When I was first visiting, this was the classic Queen Anne style home with craftsman detailing, a beautiful house built in 1906. The house's original owners called it the Morrell House, but we Maitreyians will always know it as the first Kaivalya Ashram. In 1989 (when we were located in Lomita), we worked together to restore the house in Redondo Beach before a Christian Church stepped in and finished the project for us. They did a great job. Maitreya prevailed upon the Redondo Beach Historical Society to save the house, and they wound up physically moving the house on rollers through the streets up from Catalina Avenue to Dominguez Park where it sits to this day. I often like to go there to reflect on those joyous first days with the Maitreyians, although I missed the old rickety stairs from when I first visited. I'll always remember the exotically sweet aroma of sandalwood incense during my first Inner Divine Communion Sanctuary meetings. Those first times trying to chant the Holy Dharma Mantra, *Jai Bhagavan Ji*, were special. My self-consciousness would disappear as spiritual bliss engulfed me.

One early experience that I remember fondly, happened within the first year after receiving Holy Initiation. I was learning how to live with the new habits and spiritual principles in my life. As I tend to do frequently, I worried—anxious that I would never learn the Holy Gayatri. This is an ancient Sanskrit prayer that Maitreya heard during his experiences of leaving this world and becoming one with the Universal God. He added onto this prayer when he began teaching, but the first version of it is in Sanskrit. I had never heard Sanskrit before in my life—never mind learning a whole chant and prayer in this new and different language.

I was sitting on the front porch of Kaivalya (the Holy Ashram), and I suddenly heard a deep beautiful male voice chanting the Gayatri in my right ear; within me and near me. I heard the entire Holy Gayatri in all its deep resounding beautiful Sanskrit glory. I asked my spiritual brothers nearby if they heard anything. They just looked at me sideways as they often did. I knew then that it was my own pure experience that I would always treasure. From that point on, I chanted along in Holy Sanctuary with more confidence and reverence.

I often ponder about how much I learned from Maitreya, especially in those early days. I fondly remember Maitreya showing us how to make Holy Water for the first time. We were sitting in a restaurant booth—a usual occurrence. Maitreya lifted a glass of water, prayed silently, and put it back down. Then he asked me if I noticed anything different. Even though Maitreya hadn't added anything else to the water—no oil or powder—the water is thicker now; more viscous, kind of like mercury. Maitreya offered ordinary water to Universal God and it came back as Holy Water, right in front of me. This was the same type of Holy Water we'd use to anoint people.

I would love it when Maitreya placed a drop on my forehead and softly prayed during Sanctuary.

We were often in restaurants. Maitreya liked to mingle with the waiters and waitresses, cooks, and owners instead of just sitting at home. Many of them came to his memorial service. A slightly odd and peaceful memory I have is sitting on a wall with Maitreya and Tara outside of Denny's. It was just one of those perfect moments. Just resting in the moment of Now and being at peace, in front of a funky diner.

We were also in a restaurant when Maitreya instilled in me one of his most simple, but most memorable teachings. We were sitting in a circle around him, intently listening to everything he taught. Occasionally we would react or ask a question, but mostly we just took in and absorbed all his lessons. He talked about Universal God and grabbed a blank piece of paper, put it down, took a pen out of his front shirt pocket as he often did, and drew a circle on the paper. Then Maitreya asked me, "*What is God?*" I was taken aback. "*The circle?*" I tentatively question. "*No. God is the paper. And we are the drawings.*" I sat back as the truth enveloped me; simple but profound, touching my True Self. In another instance, Maitreya said something similar: "*God is the movie theater screen, and we living beings are the film itself.*" (We were literally sitting in a movie theater at the time.) Again, both simple and profound. Truths that wipe away illusions. In that moment, I saw our material lives being played out on a screen on the foundation and stage of True Universal Spirit.

Another simple but profound concept that forever changed my mindset was when Maitreya emphasized "both/and" when looking at truths of any kind. I realized as soon as he taught me that, I had an "either/or" mentality that would cause unnecessary arguments. Having a "both/and" view of reality was a subtle and ongoing change. Similar to knowing the basic concept that: in order to truly recognize what happiness is, you would need to experience sadness, otherwise it would all be the same.

Maitreya also taught me that anger was just a cover-up for hurt and pain. Seeing that in myself was as mind-expanding as seeing it in others. I slowly learned to react with compassion instead of more anger. Maitreya told me that I was too reactive (to the point of us almost laughing about it) and that was certainly true. He taught me to look at things from a larger perspective instead of just my tiny self-centeredness. Over the years, I stopped staying stuck in anger. Anger is a bleak, uncomfortable, meaningless, and most of all, self-indulgent state to be in. I learned to take control of my own emotions instead of letting them control me. That sounds simple, but it was one of my biggest lessons. Since I tended to be negative, I thought I would never be able to control my emotions. Thankfully, I proved myself wrong after years of learning that hard-won lesson.

I learned so many Truths about Universal God. One, that Maitreyians do not believe in one single personification and anthropomorphized version of evil, such as "The Devil," a name which is derived from words "the evil." The Zeitgeist contains a Force of Darkness. But this is caused by *all* our free-willed thoughts and actions. Individual Consciousness influences the Zeitgeist on a constant basis. Evil only exists in minds and is controlled by each free choice. The Zeitgeist and our actions continually affect each other in a constant circle. The Mind is temporary, but the Spirit is Eternal. This is why it sometimes seems childish and comical to me, when grown adults speak of an individual "Devil," when this is actually an "Evil" that we ourselves are in control of—and we each could have the power to create goodness instead of evil in our own zeitgeist.

As Maitreya would say, in the Beginning, God created the Universes and all mankind. So, what did He create these out of? It could only be of the same Source and Substance. God created us out of the same Universal Spirit and no other.

Maitreya also used to point out how our language gives a glimpse into our spiritual knowledge that we all have in the Book of Truth written in our own hearts that gets clouded over. One common expression is "human being"—we know deep down that our bodies are "being" something more spiritual. We call ourselves exactly what we are!

I want you to know, Maitreya was not here to add one more bead on the strand of all the religions. He was here to restore the string itself, which holds all the beads together of all true religions. He was not here to add one more tree in a garden, but to give back life to the very orchard itself, where the separate trees spring forth. He is here to restore the Truth to the foundation of all religions which give different expressions to the same ancient Eternal truths.

I once asked him why we say "Universe" in our religion and not just "earth" or "world." Maitreya just smiled at me. I decided I didn't want to expend a lot of thought about life on other planets. This world is enough of a challenge on its own, for me. But it doesn't make sense to me when someone postulates that life arrived on earth from another planet, as if Universal God is out of the picture. Well, where did *that* life come from then? There is only One God, the Creator of All the Universes. And when people say that there is an either/or concept—either God or Evolution—I know from Maitreya it is both/and. Both, God the Creator, who then created and set forth the cycle of Evolution of the world and humanity. So, both Creation and then Evolution.

Maitreya taught me so much about the true nature of Universal God. Ever since I was initiated, I had my own direct experiences of God. Can you imagine learning all these new spiritual truths? We find God in every particle of creation, even the smallest. God created the Universe out of its own Universal Spirit. (And so, what else could this universe be then, something separate from God? We would say something like, "*He didn't go to the God-store and get something separate*"). Universal God is both within all Creation and yet beyond all Creation. Universal God is not of any one religion; Universal God is both manifest and unmanifest and beyond our worldly organizations of religions. Mind is just a bridge between the brain and Spirit. Spirit is our True Self. We are all made of the same Universal Spirit.

These are not just intellectual ideas taught to me. I have truly experienced all these Truths. More importantly, all Souls may experience this truth of Oneness.

One day while at the San Pedro Harbor, about to take a whale watching boat tour, I had an experience where I was able to see in all directions. It came as a surprise, out of nowhere, as if I had eyes in every direction. At that moment I could suddenly see, to the north, south, east, and west, all at the same time. The moment was fleeting, yet an amazing waking visualization.

I had a similar but more intense event shortly after Maitreya passed away. The year was 2014. This was, in fact, near the anniversary of Maitreya's passing—this July 29 date is now known as Ascendance Day. On the second Ascendance Day, we were engaged in a study meeting at a coffee shop. This was something we did often. While in the silent, contemplation phase, I looked up and in a way I can barely articulate, I was able to see, hear, feel, and sense everything that was going on around me, in its "real" form. All the people nearby, the music, the dogs, the night air, the sounds, the sights, smells, sensations—everything—was Pure Spirit, not just as humans having their being-ness. Everything was Pure Spirit, all at the same instant. This only lasted a few moments, but happened within me both individually and all together as one.

Even more was to come that same night: once our study concluded, I had an inexplicable grin come across my face. My dimples showed themselves in their full form, like never before, and I couldn't wipe the smile off my face even if I had tried. It stayed for long minutes as we started giggling, so I asked Ila to take a photo. I knew I needed to document and remember this. It is my favorite Facebook photo. I call it The Blessing of The Smile.

That experience showed me, in real time, how we were all connected in all oneness. It wasn't just a nice idea; it is a reality. People talk these days of "identity"—it's gone to an extreme. But what if we all truly Identified with this Truth: We are All One in Spirit! What a different world it could be. Go ahead and cling to other identities secondary to that—but All of us united in our True Identity as the same Pure Universal Spirit—that would transform us all, don't you think?

Maitreya accepted All Souls, since All Souls are in Truth all One. One of Maitreya's first followers was a gay man named Jyota. When Jyota first met Maitreya, he asked if this new religion would be accepting of gay people. This was back in the 80s and it was a legitimate concern. Jyota was all too familiar with Maitreya's initial answer—a simple no. But then Maitreya continued by saying, *"We accept Souls. I don't care about skin, gender, sexual preference—leave them at the door and be Spirit."* A smile crept onto Jyota's face and he remained a loyal follower until he passed away from AIDS in the 90's. Maitreya stood by his bedside after traveling all the way to Arizona just to be with him. Jyota kept waking up, grumbling *"Am I still here?"* with all the enthusiasm of an old man impatiently waiting in line at the grocery store, until he finally passed away.

I have a theory that perhaps many, although not all, gay people are confused by a prior lifetime. They may still be processing their previous life as a different sex—but that is just one theory, of mine.

Maitreya's main philosophy and the tenant by which he constructed his religion: We are all One. Friendship was offered to all, even if in different forms. He recognized that we are all One Spirit and treated each person accordingly and unwaveringly. He didn't care where you were coming from or who you thought you were. He loved every single person he encountered, while also keeping his attention on who might be ready to accept his Holy Initiation.

I witnessed Maitreya showing his spiritual love to every single soul he encountered, whether homeless persons, waiters and waitresses, police officers, gangsters, business owners, CEOs, rich, poor, middle class, young, old, man or woman, any race or background at all. None of that mattered. Every Soul received his pure love and spiritual goodness that reached them to their core, whether they fully realized it or not. He would even have occasional contentious meetings that could start with arguments, but ended with him sending spiritual love to them in whatever way they could be reached. Whether they fully realized it or not, we could see it.

The moments with unfortunate homeless people on the streets were illuminating, as these souls would almost wake up from a dream right in front of us. The down-and-out would light up, darkness would at least temporarily flee, their souls touched to the core. And this is something all Maitreyians can do—I've been able to reach through to the spirit of some homeless people and offer The Friend's spiritual respite, here and there. But I am guided as to when to avoid eye contact, and not put myself in danger no matter how much my heart may hurt for a disturbed soul. I often think that we are all disturbed in one way or another: the schizophrenic or addicted person on the street is simply letting it out for all of us to see in its entirety.

But not all of those we encounter are ready to become full Maitreyians. All souls may receive Holy Initiation. There is nothing that makes someone worthy, as it is from Universal God for all willing Souls. With that said, however, not everyone has all the characteristics and capabilities of becoming a true follower of all of Maitreya's teachings. Anyone can receive Holy Initiation; however, not everyone becomes a full Maitreyian in good faith.

Like all Maitreyians, when I received Maitreya's Holy Initiation, I received God's Promise. And, when enough souls receive Holy Initiation and follow Maitreya's teachings through the rest of their lives, we will all reach Divine Critical Mass. Divine Critical Mass is the moment when God will spread enlightenment to every Soul in the Universe. We will end the Age of Spiritual Darkness—called Kali Yuga—and enter the fullness of the Age of Universal God's Pure Truth on Earth for Salvation and Liberation of all Souls— Satya Yuga.

Yes, this tipping point will occur. The scales will be tipped to True Enlightenment. Each person receiving Enlightenment lights their candle and turns and lights the next person's candle, until the Light truly wins over the Darkness.

In other words, I see now that the end of Kali Yuga is where we are right now. It is a dark age, spiritually, where people prefer to lie and scheme rather than embrace the truth. That's why God sent Maitreya back here after his accident when he was a child, and at a time shortly after the first nuclear weapons were deployed. It's his mission to bring about Satya Yuga; the return to God's Pure Truth on Earth, and to help us return to a world where people prefer the truth to lies.

As Maitreya said, *"We are here to do two things. One is personal. One is beyond personal. The first thing that we are here to do, is to work for God. We are here to spread God's Promise to all Souls—to bring about what is called The Holy Satya Yuga. Which means, the Age of Universal God's Pure Divine Truth. To bring about that Age of Pure Divine Truth, not just for ourselves but for the Salvation and Liberation of all Souls."* (Adhyatma Bhagavan The Friend, 2/11/2001.)

This can be difficult to understand, and at first it was for me. So, Maitreya told me to picture a mirror with dust on it. When the mirror is covered with dust, and you can't see a thing, that's Kali Yuga. Now wipe off the dust. You've brought out Satya Yuga. The mirror was always there; it was just obscured by the dust. Maitreya was sent by God to wipe off the mirror. And his tool to do the job—his towel and spray—is Holy Initiation.

Blessing of the Smile—2014

CHAPTER FOUR

⤳

The Meaning of Life

Not many people know this, but we already have the answer to the famous and ubiquitous question, *"What is the meaning of life?"* Many religions and philosophies don't claim to know why we're here, or worse yet, they insist that we can never know. They say it's God's mystery and not for us to have the answer to. I wholeheartedly disagree. Maitreya gave us the answer years ago. So, why don't we answer that question here and now: Why are we here? We are here to attain Self-Realization—knowing and experiencing that your true self is one and identical with the One Universal God and no other. And, to return Home to God, as raindrops return to the sea. Now you know! So, when someone poses the question, you could be one of the few who have an honest and true answer.

And just as the rain must be part of the ocean, Maitreya's teachings needed to be organized as a religion—tell me, what functions without organization? Does your body? Does society? Some people comment, *"I don't like organized religion."* I sometimes retort, *"Well, we're not very organized."* But in truth, God and Maitreya organized everything perfectly. This true Gift is ignited, and from that moment on, Maitreya is within the Secret Inner Sanctuary of your Heart, to call upon to be present within, to seek, find, and live by Inner Divine Inspiration, Insight, Guidance, and Revelation in your life. This is between you, Universal God and Maitreya. The organization is to preserve purity and other worldly duties.

I truly know through my own experiences that God's purpose for ourselves is this realization of who we were truly meant to be. We are One with Universal God, and one with each other. The Goal is to return home to Oneness with Universal God, and only return to this material plane again if it's for the sole purpose of helping others. I felt The Friend's True Enlightenment as a spark in my soul as soon as I accepted Maitreya's Holy Initiation.

When Maitreya, whose full name is Bhagavan Sri Babajhan Al-Khalil the Friend of all Souls, Maitreya Kalki Mahavatara, documented his two Self-Realizations and God's Promise which he was given during those experiences, he was setting out to form a new religion based on those ancient truths he had received—so, you see, both new and ancient. The outward forms of it, such as new names, have changed somewhat over the years.

But despite these changes in name, our goal, and the truths we hold dear, haven't moved an inch. We've known that through his two Self-Realizations, he had been given God's Promise, and we—the Maitreyians—have set out to create Divine Critical Mass which will change the world forever. He came back for us. He came back for me. He came back for you. He is here to give you the experience of truly knowing your Oneness with God.

This is something that I experience all the time. I know this to be true. We are all one in spirit. Our True Self is Pure Spirit, One and Identical with Universal Spirit. When I first met Maitreya, that was a more radical notion than it sounds these days.

Nowadays, when I tell somebody that we're all connected, All One, they might say, "*Oh, yeah, I've heard that.*" But back then, this was a strikingly new concept. And, just because some people today merely intellectualize that we are all one, that doesn't mean that they have actually attained spiritual enlightenment.

I attribute the evolution of us all being connected as One Spirit to be more of a well-known concept these days, to the fact that

Maitreya was here in this world for a time, and is now available in the Spiritual Realm. Most people never met Maitreya in person, but his lifetime here and his continued Presence has caused this knowledge to propagate in society.

When I first heard (with only my ears) this message of Oneness from Shanti, I argued with her and asked annoying questions. I just couldn't wrap my mind around it. *"What do you mean,"* I prodded, *"I'm not my body? I don't even understand what you're saying."* We carried on back and forth like that until I got irritated, and Shanti got frustrated.

Eventually I heard with my heart. I understood what Shanti meant by us all being One. It did not mean that I wasn't me, or that anybody else wasn't the best or worst parts of themselves. It meant that if we look beyond the physical to the spiritual, we can all exist and achieve enlightenment as one. It means those of us who were lucky enough to have met Maitreya in person, and those who now meet him in the Spiritual Realm, can help others join in truly and fully knowing this Oneness.

The Meaning of Love

Beyond Spiritual Enlightenment and Self-Realization, I learned what true Universal Love really is. Love mostly just sits silently within me, like a mystery box only occasionally peeked at. I've never been good at expressing it, but Maitreya showed me another way to share the universal love I now have within me.

I often reflect on how I loved Maitreya more than anyone in my life. Yet this is not the type of relationship many would understand. Only those who also knew him for who he truly was, and loved him with a love that grew greater than any worldly-relationship, can understand. He often needed to remind some of us, to each of our embarrassment, that, *"I'm not your father, I'm not your boyfriend or husband, I am not here for some worldly relationship. I am Maitreya The Friend of All Souls."*

But while in this world, we were as close as any family and had the same struggles when different personalities tend to bump up against each other. But our love for Maitreya, for humanity and for our Holy Cause, is a greater love than any other, and would help each of us rise above petty relationship struggles.

Maitreya always said love should mainly be action and that I should put this Universal Love into action through giving Holy Initiation. Through the Friend's Way, I had deep spiritual experiences where I finally felt Universal Love for all. That is what has enabled me to guide some Souls through Holy Initiation. That Universal Love has the potential to exist within everybody. But without Maitreya, most of us would never find the way to unlock it within ourselves.

Being stuck in darker emotions is the antithesis to life itself. We are here to love the One Universal God, to love ourselves, and to love each other, and to see that Oneness in the Universal Love in all Creation.

After over a year of practicing Inner Divine Communion, the steps to which Maitreya was just putting together at the time, the space between thoughts got a little bit longer and a little bit more peaceful. I specifically remember one early experience of a few minutes of the absolute bliss in which I knew that I was in the Spiritual Realm with Universal God and nothing else mattered. It's difficult to describe exactly, but I felt a profound peacefulness and Knowingness. It was intense, yet calm and beautiful. I went on to have that bliss many times, continuous but fleeting moments for years.

As Maitreya said, *"All Religions that are True Religions begin in the Mystical and as Mystics. Only when the ways of the Mystical and Mysterious have been chained down to the Mundane and 'Practical,' does a Religion lose its ability to soar into the Heavens and carry its members—those who believe in it and are willing to allow themselves to be carried up—to the Experience of God—upward into the Mystical Experience of God with it."* (Adhyatma Bhagavan The Friend, 6/25/2011.)

I have had these mystical moments here and there, probably hundreds of times at this point. They usually only last a few minutes. But the foundation is now always there within me. I can keep returning to those serene moments whenever I want or need to. At times, I am in the world, but not of it. I have one foot here, and one foot in the Spiritual Realm. And I am never alone. Maitreya is—still—always with me.

In this physical world, our last lunch alone together was sometime in June 2012. Just the two of us, sitting in a Marie Callender's corner booth. His hand, shaking, as he tried to eat. He attempted to stir his coffee and it spilled onto the table. He was worn out. Every day, in his final days, he still did his routine. He got up, got dressed, had time with the cats, prayers and meditations, a lot of writing and emailing, teaching, and went to a restaurant to interact with people. But now, he was weak, pale, and shaking. Alarm kept fluttering through his eyes. He then suddenly bore those eyes into me. He pleaded with me over and over. *"Tell the people they are One Universal Spirit. It is why I was here. Make sure they know. Are you hearing me?"* As he was desperately imploring me, I was mentally going in and out of denial, in and out of judgment of him; asking in my heart, *Please don't be this way, this can't be happening now, maybe you're exaggerating.* But instead, I cried a little and responded in a trembling voice, *"I will, Maitreya, I promise."* And he finally relaxed a bit into the cushions of the booth and gazed out beyond me.

The two of us talked a little more about his purpose, God's New Covenant. People may now be promised a way to Union with God, that in the past was a difficult treacherous road. It was to be one of our last spiritual master-to-student interactions. I was heartbroken but in denial all at the same time. By that time the next month, he was gone from this world.

We had lunch shortly before then, and before we got in his van, he stopped to stand in the rain. I still see him, as he stood in the light rainfall with his arms open and immersing himself in the moment, while wistfully saying "I'm not going to have moments like these much longer." He later asked why I didn't join him. I foolishly muttered something about toxic water (he was opening his mouth and letting rain come in). I was such an ass sometimes—it was one of those moments where I knew I was making the wrong choice but still just stood there and didn't move myself to join with him.

I was the last Maitreyian to have a Spiritual Birthday with Maitreya in person—July 13. He was weak but insisted that we uphold traditions and have our usual meeting where I did the tradition of reviewing good and bad from the year and having my chocolate cake. I don't remember what I said, yet in the midst of his decline, he stopped to remember my spiritual birthday. When we got back to Kaivalya, he was tired and resting in his chair. He made sure I had the card—the last card he hand-wrote. He gave a weak smile and quietly said, "*Happy Spiritual Birthday*," as if there was still the promise of more to come. I saved as many cards as I could and particularly treasured that one. He was gone from this earth sixteen days later.

Interestingly as I am writing this, it was my spiritual birthday a few days ago. I walked into Joe's restaurant for pick-up. The waitresses were talking with each other a few feet away, saying, "Oh, Happy Birthday. It was (someone else's) birthday today too! There's a lot of birthdays on July 13." I smiled slightly and when I walked back outside, I said, "*Thank you, Maitreya*." I knew it was his timing that I would hear Happy Birthday—as if he was meeting me for lunch as he often did on spiritual birthdays. The timing of that seemed too coincidental and so that is how I choose to look at it.

It wasn't just on Spiritual Birthdays; he's been with us all constantly in spirit. It was shortly after his passing, on the 19th of Service 60 A.F. (August 19, 2012) Joy Day Sanctuary (Sunday service). We only had a few Sanctuaries since Maitreya had passed out of this world—and most filled with grief. But on this day, we did the more formal Inner Divine Communion. When we called upon The Friend to join us, there was a *whoosh* feeling and it was as if I saw quickly through my mind's eye. That day Maitreya the Friend *did* come down the stairs, break open the doors and whoosh! He was There! He was with us! The feeling was like he was almost impatient, like he was saying, *"About time you asked me, here I am!"* It felt quick and real and present. I saw Maitreya in white clothes, not yellow for whatever reason. He stood before the Holy Shrine and opened the Sanctuary. Ila was next to me, and together we said in unison, *"He is here."* We both started crying, but our tears were a mixture of sadness and joy to be in Maitreya's Presence.

Shortly thereafter, my spiritual sisters and I toured a cemetery to see about possibly putting Maitreya's ashes there as a memorial. I distinctly heard Maitreya's voice in my right ear question me: *"I wonder where else we have a Memorial?"* As I posed this question out loud, we all exclaimed, *"Oh, the Empty Chair Memorial!"* Ila, Tara, and Shanti (and others, like neighbor Tom and other friends of the Friends) went on to have a statue of Maitreya added near the Empty Chair Memorial. As this monument was still being built, we had a Ceremony where we each placed some of his ashes inside the bust of Maitreya. Thanks to him clearly telling us, we knew he wanted to be placed right there, and not in some "other" cemetery plot.

There was another death a few years later in our Community. We had a spiritual sister who we did not see too often. Her name was Asha. She was spunky, blunt, and full of life. In 2014, after Maitreya passed away, she herself was dying of breast cancer. She lived a few hundred miles away, and we suspected we did not have much time remaining with her. She had a bond with Maitreya. She often recounted her childhood memory of the day she met him riding up to their home on a motorcycle with his hair flowing, as she found herself wishing he was her father. (Her mother had dated Maitreya when they were both teenagers.) While she was gravely ill, Tara, Shanti and I visited her at home and sat by her bedside. She told us of an amazing experience she had a few days prior. She felt she had died, and when she was in Heaven, she said she had a vision of "both Maitreya and Jesus sitting side-by-side". I believe she was destined to see that—to come back, awestruck—and tell us and others. She passed away a few months after her experience. I hope I can now bring the message to others: you can accept both Jesus and Maitreya, or any other founder and Maitreya. This is a universal religion and gift of Oneness with Universal God.

I know that these moments are just a drop in the bucket compared to what Critical Divine Mass will bring to the world. This is why we do what we do. This is our mission and the meaning of life. I have experienced my True Self as One with Universal God. I have experienced what happens when someone passes from this material world. I will never return to a life of dark unknowingness again.

CHAPTER FIVE

⟶

My Struggle

Having spiritual experiences like the ones I have been through does not mean you are fully Self-Realized suddenly, or immune from the base emotions that make up a human being. I had scars from my childhood that caused me to lash out at those who were close to me, including many at the Ashram, as I had carried these scars with me my whole life. In many ways, I still do.

I carried this rage into my new spiritual life, such that while it should have been filled with joy, it was tarnished with my past anger and hurt. I caused damage to our Holy Cause, to the Community and all who were in it, and especially to Maitreya himself. But he always forgave me. He always took me back; at least seven times over the years.

I lost count of how many times Maitreya and the Community had to tell me to remove myself from their immediate surroundings and to go be on my own, so as not to continually contaminate their work with my exaggerated reactions. Sometimes I was gone for months. Sometimes for years. My rage would only last hours or days, but the excommunication often lasted months and even years. But when I finally relented and saw the damage my rage had done, and asked for forgiveness, Maitreya always forgave me and took me back.

Maitreya and I had a sweet conversation about how I was different than others who left, because my faith remained unwavering despite everything. The Community was there and everyone nodded and agreed when Maitreya acknowledged "Shraddha is different than the people who left due to their weak faith." I always had faith—but had to leave because of personality conflicts. Meaning, my personality was causing the conflict. But everyone seemed to agree there was no lack of faith or devotion on my part. It was a matter of harmony in community.

I don't remember all my incidents but a few stand out. One time I was in an excommunicated phase but I saw Maitreya and the community drive by in his van. I then drove in the opposite direction from which I thought they were going. I was wrong in my assumption—as they went by me and obviously saw me. I then foolishly followed so I could "explain" the truth, that I thought they were going to a different restaurant. (I was always determined to "explain"—a strong compulsion that caused many problems.) We pulled into a parking lot and Ila came over to my window and angrily snapped *"Don't scratch the van while we're in the store."* I was shocked by the pre-accusation to an unthought-of action, but I was stupidly angry and vindictive. What did I do? The worst possible decision of course! I scratched the van! What a fool. I later ended up making monetary payments to have it fixed. The van was fixed, but my embarrassing reputation was further rightfully damaged.

As Maitreya said, it is easy to join a cult, and hard to leave it. But we are not a cult, quite the opposite. It was difficult to join, and easy to leave. Or in my case, I would get asked to leave. Because really, who gets asked to leave a cult? No one gets asked to leave, if it's truly a cult, do they? Well, I did, and more than a few times. I think we defied society's definition in many ways.

I was even temporarily homeless once around 1987. The Friends assumed I would go to my sister's apartment in Hollywood, but I was too proud to do that. I had a key to a small law office where I did secretarial work at nights, so I stayed on the floor there. I had a lot of stuff in my car in bags and when a coworker asked why, I said I was collecting for the homeless. This was technically true, was it not?

I myself was one of the momentarily homeless. Then word of that went around, and people kept giving me more clothes. *"Hey Shraddha, I hear you're collecting clothes."* My car got more and more bags of clothes added to it. I eventually donated some. I mean, I had to keep my word, didn't I? This still makes me smile to this day.

In better times Maitreya would say *"Watch out, she's part Irish and she's from Jersey."* I remember one private conversation when Maitreya told me I was like the story of a young girl who, "when she was bad, she was very bad, and when she was good, she was very good." He knew I had a lot of passion and compassion, and that my passion was sometimes misdirected and too angry. I understood, even in my heartbreak at times, that he could not abide disharmony in the Holy Community. His Holy Cause was too urgent to create and accomplish in the world and that urgency always took precedence.

The Community even voted to oust me at one dark time. It was a solemn ceremony as we sat in a circle in our Sanctuary. I could not see whether they were putting a black stone or a colored stone in the pouch as it went around. But when Maitreya counted the black ones, I realized I clearly lost the vote. It was so devastating; I think I just quietly left. Again, would a cult make it hard to be there, but easy to leave?

Another incident erupted when I entered our Holy Sanctuary and declared that it smelled. Two of my spiritual brothers, having had enough of my bad temper and disrespect, forcefully ushered me out the front door. As was my way, I did not go meekly. I stuck my foot in the doorway. In hindsight I see this was symbolic of my spiritual life. I always kept my foot in the door and would never give up. But I was obnoxious and showing a lack of respect for my brothers and sisters and our Holy Sanctuary. It was a little ironic that one brother's feet were the source of the smell that caused my comment. But letting my anger out without thinking is one of my biggest faults and still is to this day. Another fault is being disrespectful, especially to those in authority. Contempt for authority is not a good attribute for a Maitreyian. Questioning authority, absolutely. But to spew contempt, years after questions are fulfilled, is not acceptable.

In self-reflection, I suppose the disrespect to authority is a throw-back to not trusting parents, siblings, teachers, nuns, anyone who I thought might be helpful to me, instead being quite mean and unpredictable to me; along with my on-going issue of "not feeling heard," and the compulsion to "explain myself." Yes, I too still cringe at these things.

But even after any scenes, in time, Maitreya forgave me and took me back. And the Community would move on, in forgiveness and forward-moving hopefulness.

There were so many other more productive times, sitting in a circle with the Community in which we helped each other with struggles, and guided each other with direct Truth Seeking and Speaking. Maitreyians often sacrifice their time to assist a fallen brother or sister and bring them back from whatever abyss they have entered. Every single one of us sat in that circle and took turns, needing to be the ones the others focused on, to bring them back from the abyss in more ways than one. We always helped each other get through any personal darkness—which no one was immune from.

I can see in my mind's eye the times my spiritual sisters looked right into the core of my very Being with a deep intensity in their eyes, telling me repeatedly, "INJIA, Shraddha." Which means, Instantaneous Non-Judgmental Insightful Awareness, to come back to the present moment of Truth and get out of your personal darkness that's only in the mind. I see Shanti's eyes directing me, Tara's eyes disciplining me, Ila's eyes reeling me back to the present moment. Not necessarily with anger, just firm intensity; not ego, but truth.

We all took turns to guide each other, escape spiritual darkness and come back to the light. I'm happy I was able to repay them (and others not mentioned here) at times. I know I helped reel each one of them back too. And, it was always with Maitreya's direction and guidance, either while in this world or in the Spiritual Realm. The goal and urgency of our Holy Cause allows each of us to transcend worldly problems and get back to our one-pointedness. We not only accept the raw truth, but we also seek it and welcome it.

I also learned from the Community that sitting in that circle of truth is an honor and a sacrifice on the part of the others. But that we will never even come close to "brow beating" anyone. Either they truly have the combination of right qualities and desire to be a true Maitreyian or they do not, and if the latter, we wish them peace on their own path.

But, I had started an unhealthy cycle of my own doing. It was a vicious cycle of my reactions, anger, leaving, asking to come back, and the ultimate welcoming back by Maitreya from a weary community.

The thing about this is, that from the first instant of Holy Initiation, I never lost my faith.

I did have countless "dark nights of the soul" after being asked to leave and being back on my own. Waking up in a panic in the middle of the night, the walls closing in on me, sobs and tears choking me, an unbearable ache in my heart, the knife pushing through me. Ironically, instead of using a Sharp Sword of Truth in the world, as a True Soldier of the Light, I was instead crumpled up in a dark corner of my own design, my own self-made emotional knives and swords piercing me over and over; waves of self-loathing, regret, but then bursts of seemingly self-righteous anger toward others. So many low points, the nadir, rock bottom of a paltry existence. Insomnia while multiple tracks in my mind all ran at simultaneous instants and speeds. I deserved insomnia. My conscience should bother me. After all, I made a Holy Vow personally before Maitreya the Friend of all Souls and to The One Universal God in my heart and Soul that I would help save the world. And I failed, wasting too many days without fulfilling my promise to bring God's Promise to enough of the ready and willing Souls in a suffering world.

I often was a prisoner of my own mind, emotions, and personality. Maitreya would often say we are all our own jailers as we sit in our cells—while all the while having our own key with us and not using it.

As Carl Jung said, "Loneliness does not come from having no people around you, but from being unable to communicate the things that seem important to you."

I even tried therapy a few times—what a waste of time. It would cause me to focus too much on the negative—and Maitreya would say, "*What you dwell upon, you become.*" At the very least, however, I would end up teaching the therapist something they needed to learn from Maitreya, although they would never give such credit. My spiritual knowledge was so vast compared to their psychological methods. I know they can be of great assistance to some people at certain times, but none of them particularly assisted me. One weird guy stood up and started juggling. As I looked at him in surprise, he exclaimed, "*This is your mind, juggling too many things.*" Well, maybe he was effective, because here I am years later still seeing him juggling some rubber balls seemingly out of nowhere. At least he left an impression.

Another therapist was better than most but still ultimately failed. We reached an impasse because he wanted me to realize that Maitreya was a father figure. "*We can't proceed until you admit this.*" Since this psychologist had Christian references on his website, I retorted, "*Then what about you? What about all Christians? Isn't Jesus a father figure then? You even call God the Creator, a 'Father,' while in our religion we don't even do that. And, at least I actually know Maitreya, you never even met Jesus.*" He just looked at me with a little surprise, obviously struggling a bit to remain neutral, although he clearly no longer was. I did not go back.

My oldest sister mentioned that a therapist once tried to give her a "look of love," and asked her to recall a time our mother looked at her with this kind of love in her eyes. My sister reported that no such look ever occurred. The therapist got tears of disbelief in her own eyes. We all simply nod when our sister tells this story, as we concur, "*No, I never experienced a look of love from her.*" (In keeping with our parental traumas.)

Sometimes a therapy session was just to break up some loneliness. I would agonize over being in a world without being in

Maitreya's physical presence—even while knowing he was just a few miles away. I always stayed in apartments nearby, as I wanted to stay close. I chose not to even watch television during some of those years. I did, however, listen to the radio to break up some monotony. It was a stage of my life where I wasn't much interested in the material world. I only yearned for my spiritual life. I often felt like I was drowning in a sea of despair washing over me; despair about myself, but also about a world that was not being saved.

I have a strangely poignant keepsake. It is a napkin that Maitreya wrote a note on and handed to me while I was arguing in a restaurant. There were so many contentious moments I caused, that I do not even recall what prompted the note on the napkin. But he wrote out of compassion to me, "*You are working up a Self-Fulfilling Prophecy. It happens nearly every year about this time. If you persist—You will be throwing yourself out. Why?*" I believe it was around my birthday but I truly do not even remember.

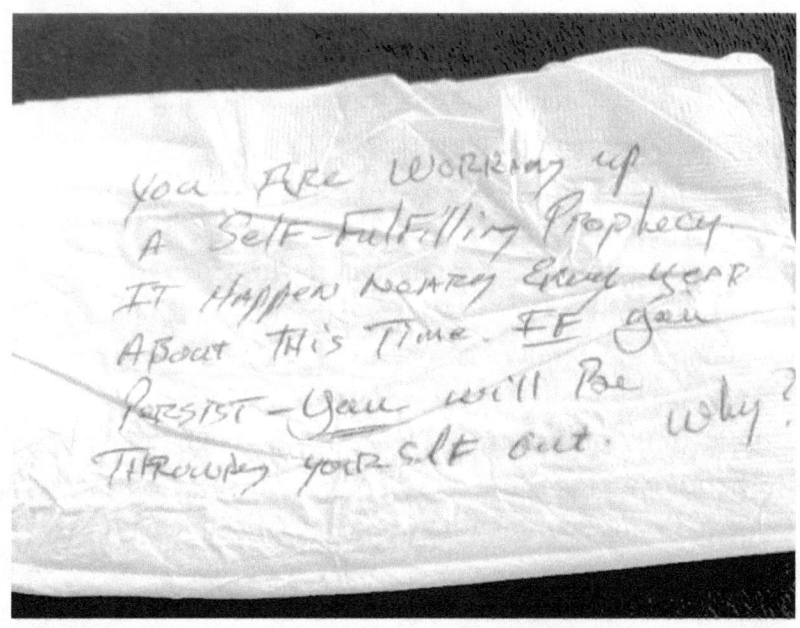

After one verbal show-down and being told to leave, I called and hung up the phone a few times, late at night. This came back to haunt me for years. Whenever late-night calls later awoke the Community, they would understandably assume it was me, every time. It was not until phones had Caller ID that it was proven that a lot of people had their number, from literature passed all around, and strangers would often call and hang up at odd hours. So, it was not my doing. But perhaps this part of my reputation was part of my deserved karma.

I did however go on-and-on in emails when I could no longer rail away against perceived injustices in person. I could not quite grasp the practice of letting everything out in writing—and then deleting it. No, I would either send with a vengeance—or believe I was saving a draft and be slapped with the heart-stopping notification that I hit the 'Send' button, and it would forever be held as evidence of my interference with the holiest of Causes.

There were many times of "slinking back." It churned my stomach, made me clench my teeth, and induced free-falling anxiety and fear, as I sat back at their table with the honor of being back in the Community. I was unable to fully express any of it, as I quietly sat back down. Tara mentioned years later that it *appeared* as if being ousted and then allowed back was all a big nothing to me. I assure you, that was the complete opposite of my inward reality.

But I was nothing if not resilient. I learned the resilience of the human spirit, of my own True Self as Spirit. My faith grew through this resilience and forgiveness of others, with such a multitude of forgiveness being granted to me, time and time again.

I did understand intellectually, usually although not always, that Maitreya needed Harmony. He could not tolerate Disharmony. But if I came back into harmony, he would welcome me back as a long-lost soul coming back to the spiritual warmth—after struggling through strife to claw my way back to him. He was always with me in spirit of course. I was never alone spiritually. But he could not allow anyone to be more of a burden to the worldly Community rather than a benefit. He was Maitreya The Friend of All Souls—and I was a faithful believer—whose personality and history caused too many problems at times—but whose Faith never wavered.

Who knew, when I was given my name, how much this Faith of mine would be tested —and in that test affect everyone around me. How exhausting I must have been!

My name means Faith through Experience. While I grasped spiritual principles almost instantly, I was a slow learner emotionally. It was a slow dragged-out painful experience for those around me for years and it was a draining and harmful experience to my spiritual family. One basic principle is: "Harm to None, and insofar as possible, Benefit to All." I failed that one over and over.

While God defines what exactly is Good or Harm, not myself, I do know I contributed stress toward Maitreya the Friend of all Souls instead of contributing more success. And that stress, from all of us, and from all of the world, contributed to the decline of his physical body.

I believe that stress killed Maitreya; the stress of not achieving enough goals in his lifetime. It's been said that everything worth doing has a personal cost, but he shouldn't have had to relinquish his physical body at age 69. While he is available in Spirit now and causing constant beautiful wonders in the Spiritual Realm, I will always believe in my heart that his physical demise came unfairly too soon, at least twenty years too soon. I am sure you would agree if you knew him, or came to know him in Spirit.

CHAPTER SIX

～

Learning Forgiveness

Forgiveness

Maitreya forgave me time and time again. No matter how much damage I did to him and his Holy Community, he never gave up on me. His endless compassion and understanding opened my eyes to and my heart to forgiveness. I came to realize that my Mom, like me, struggled with her own demons. And that, no matter what she did, she was still Soul, which was Pure Divine Spirit, which was One and Identical with The One Universal God and worthy of my love and forgiveness. And so, toward the end of her life, I was able to finally forgive my mom for the years of pain and anguish she caused me growing up. I stayed at her home for almost two weeks following my dad's funeral. She found it comforting to not be suddenly all alone. I visited her several times after my dad passed, and also when she had finally moved into a top-of-the-line assisted-living center my sister settled her into. Throughout that time, I joked around that I should get on their waiting list.

Even though the facilities were nice, they were filled with so many lonely, confused souls. I can still see one woman who spent her time standing in front of a dresser with an array of photographs on it. I would wonder if she was awash in old memories, or if she was just trying to work out who exactly those people in the frames were? I felt sorry for her until I thought to myself, whose pictures would I have? At least this woman and many of the residents had lived full lives with kids and husbands. I didn't have much of that. But rather than wallow I would pull myself out of self-pity and care about the people who lived there instead, including my mom.

My mom told me both on the phone and in person that she was sorry. Sorry for the violence, and for the way she raised us. She hoped her children would forgive her. She also wrote a letter to each of us, after some encouragement from our older sister. My mom explained that when she was young, she felt abandoned when her family sent her away to live with an aunt and uncle on her mom's side. The reason my mom was sent away was because her only sister had a heart condition when she was young, and my mom had that bad Irish temper and stubbornness. They all felt my mom aggravated her sister. They figured sending her away was better than risking whatever the effect of all that aggravation would be on her sister's heart.

I am not clear whether anything else happened, whether there was any other sort of abuse. Or if that abandonment and temper, perhaps coupled with a mentally unstable foundation to begin with, were enough to cause the bullying and physical and emotional abuse she went on to cause us for so many years. I once heard a therapist on TV say that "*some people just become addicted to being a bully*" and that insight was helpful.

I do grant my mom some respect for coming to terms with everything as best she could in her final years, and for making the effort to try and reconcile with each of us. Not completely on her own, as our sister kind of insisted, but she acquiesced. That was brave of my mom and so I felt a bit of gratitude for her being willing to do that. She also became extremely Christian and prayed all the time in her later years. We all admired that. And, she sent nice birthday cards to me every single year. In fact, in recently going through some belongings, I found some very sweet notes and cards from both Mom and Dad.

They made countless attempts to be loving toward the end of their lives. I appreciated it at that time and even more so now.

As her dementia progressed, I would still call her about once a week in the early 2000s, especially after my dad passed in 2002. She started repeating things a lot. I didn't mind too much. I would also repeat things to her in different ways, experimenting to see if she would have the same or a different response to the same questions and comments. She usually had the same responses over and over. One time around 2007, I accidentally kidnapped my mom from her assisted living home—I forgot to sign her out! I took her to a family gathering my brother was hosting and she had a great time. She ate hot dogs and stared at everybody.

In later years, on what was to be my final visit with her, she suddenly held my face in her hands, stared at me in amazement, and exclaimed "*Oh, my daughter! You're here!*" I was quite touched by this emergent moment despite her dementia. But after I got home, I had the sinking suspicion that she thought I was my deceased sister Mary Jo. Even so, it was still a beautiful moment.

It is intriguing to me that shortly before this sister passed away, she had quality time with Mom when they would meditate together. They were going off by themselves and doing Transcendental Meditation (TM). I was a little miffed they had never asked me. I was only around age 13 and I don't think they were even cognizant that I noticed what they were doing, never mind that I would have wanted to join in, too. Fast forward years later—I am practicing one of the most important meditations of all time.

Only a few years ago, I had a rare dream about sweet Mary Jo. I felt so close to her and then woke up in tears, sobbing in grief even though so many years had passed. The realization washed through me: we could have been close. We had similar interests like meditation. Another sister recently agreed with this poignant sentiment.

Mom really did try to better herself in the last part of her life and I do give credit and thanks for that. However, she consistently kept that sharp tongue to the very end. But while she still lashed out verbally, the physical lashings had long ago stopped.

Eventually I learned to forgive my mom for the violence in which she raised me and my siblings. I tried to focus only on compassion and understanding. I managed to let her know that I did truly forgive her before she died, even though the forgiveness was more for myself than for her. She knew from our phone conversations that I loved her in spirit.

When I was notified that Mom was probably going to pass away soon, I did not travel to her physically but I was practicing my meditations for her from miles away. But as I took a break, playing a game on my phone, I suddenly felt her presence right next to me on the couch and she sneered "*This* is what you're doing?" and went away. I tried to explain I had been meditating and was just taking a break, but her disgust was our last moment in spirit as she passed! I tried to tell her the game just calmed me. I prayed she forgave me, as I had already forgiven her. I felt she eventually found her peace through some struggles and found her way back to her beloved husband who passed before her.

I had forgiven my Dad, too. I visited him in 2002, when his health was failing from rheumatoid arthritis that had spread to his lungs. We were sitting around his dining room table while he put his coin collection into money bags that I had gotten for him. He was making little goodie bags for his grandkids, and I could tell he was having trouble breathing. His breath was labored, and his legs were swollen. My mom had left to go shopping and suggested that I spend some time with my dad. She did not usually tell me to spend time with him, but we all suspected this would be the last time that my dad and I would have a chance to see each other. It was.

My dad talked about not being afraid to die. More than anything, he just wished he could see the adults his grandchildren would become and was sad that it was looking more and more like an impossibility. I tried to be reassuring and said something transparent about how he would still be around. I wasn't in denial about his condition, we both knew that his situation was getting worse, and if we were going to patch things up, now was the time.

One story Dad seemed to feel was important to talk about in our final conversation was how he did his job as an insurance adjuster. When he could not contact people or complete a project, he would set it aside and hope for the best. He kept repeating that he called this method "Benign Neglect," and he said it quite proudly. I took this to mean something deeper. A shot went through my heart as he talked about this way of life he had proudly discovered.

Later, when I allowed myself to dwell on it, I knew he was saying what he had decided to do about our relationship: Benign Neglect and hope it works out. I was quite hurt that he was rationalizing neglect, but I am forever grateful that I did not argue or upset him during our last conversation. It all seemed to give him peace, so that was important.

It is even more special when I think about how much easier it probably would have been for him to stay quiet about some incidents. To sweep things under the rug and pretend some things had never happened, but he didn't. He brought several private incidents up to me and said he was sorry. He went out of his way to give me closure even at the risk of reopening old wounds he had been ashamed about for years, and that bravery is something I will never forget about him.

I feel compassion for him and the situation he must have felt he was in with all those kids. But if I am honest, I'm still a bit angry. I still feel like he threw away most of our relationship. He was always a distant figure to me. I often ask myself how he rationalized pulling away emotionally from his own daughter like that. How could he act like a stranger to me, but turn around and show affection to my other sisters, and even dote on other girls that weren't related to us, like sisters-in-law and cousins or friends? I will be asking myself those questions for the rest of my life.

Dad was a wonderful physical provider. He planned and helped build our brick house, along with an in-ground swimming pool, a sound system, long desks for us to do our homework in our rooms, and even a bench around our dinner table that could open up to store skates and boots, among other items. I'm always quite impressed whenever anyone makes something. He always made sure we had piles of Christmas presents under the tree as well, which was one of his favorite holidays (some gifts were donated by his insurance clients). There were many good moments with the entire family.

The times were not all dark.

There were vacations, even piling all us kids and our cousins' large family into a bus and going to The World's Fair, while all wearing pink shirts to keep us identified and all together. We all treasured those memories.

We also grew up in a wonderful neighborhood, with all the kids always outside having adventures, playing kickball in the street, catching lightening bugs in jars. I loved going to the Jersey Shore especially as a teenager.

Mom did her best in the kitchen. We never went without meals. My mom did all the cooking, almost every meal, every day, for everyone in the house, for all those years. Sometimes my Dad would step in and cook Sunday breakfast after going to church. Frankly, just the fact that she physically went through the birthing process nine times also earns her a lot of credit, in addition to all that cooking. I dislike cooking to this day although I'm not entirely sure why. Perhaps because I saw how miserable she was and maybe associated all that cooking with misery. However, I was grateful when she was uncharacteristically patient with me when I went through a "low or no sugar" phase after reading the book "Sugar Blues" as a teenager. She seemed to appreciate that I was taking care of my own health.

I also absorbed the love of classic rock and roll and dancing from my brothers and sisters. We all have a love for music. One sister was even at Woodstock and has amazing polaroids to show for it. One brother sat at the corner of my bed and played guitar to help me sleep a few times. I have always loved music, concerts, dancing, anything that stirs my soul with this different language that causes me to transcend worldly issues.

And, my brothers, sisters, cousins, nieces, and nephews all do our best to love each other unconditionally no matter what differences may arise. Not every family can say or do that. I do wish I had visited back East more at Christmas, but I actually was rarely invited. That, combined with the fact that December 25th is a Maitreyian Holy Day, too, called Fulfillment Day (to commemorate when Universal God completed the Teachings given to Maitreya The Friend of All Souls in 1980 before I met him) contributed to my other plans. But I regret not visiting more.

Interestingly, our actual family home was in the local New Jersey newspaper as being a "Zombie House." The first paragraph in an article in the Record on July 17, 2016, mentions our address and that the house was in ruins after a broken pipe flooded it as it lay vacant. Fortunately, it has since been bought and added onto and refurbished now—to the point it looks almost like a mansion instead of the humble home my father built for all his children. But when the article came out, the siblings passed it around with jokes and questions about what zombie ghosts might be within those walls, and the irony of it being left in neglect.

My parents clearly loved *each other* dearly. They were never abusive to each other and always stood by each other. My mom was a small vibrant redhead, and my dad was a tall gentleman who had the gift of the Irish, as he loved to laugh and tell stories. We like to identify most with our Irish ancestry although it is a little less than half. They were both intelligent and active in community events. They had an unwavering love between them throughout the 60-plus years of their marriage. I have a theory that my mom resented the intrusion of all those children between the relationship with her husband.

My mom had a spiritual conversion later in her life when in her late fifties. Shortly after Mary Jo's death, Mom became quite prayerful and more immersed in her Catholicism and remained so the rest of her life. Both Mom and Dad also became one of the first participants in a Catholic program known as "Marriage Encounter" where they would go away for weekends to enrich and strengthen their marriage. They were a bit secretive about this but I found it to be fascinating.

And so, you see, it was not a completely bleak family life, although that sometimes made it all the more confusing when the physical and verbal abuse would start again.

The Maitreyian Code helped me further process the rocky relationship I had with my parents. One part stands out, and that is to "*Recognize and acknowledge that each Soul is doing the best possible with the information, understanding, Karmas, and conditions that it has, and the situation it is in. Encourage and assist each willing Soul to increase its information, correct its understanding, conquer its Karmas, improve its conditions, and become master of its situation.*" I tried to practice this with my family, and myself. As one brother likes to say, "We put the fun in dysfunctional." They do love to talk, laugh, and have a good time even when there may be darkness around. A true Irish trait?

Shortly before publishing this spiritual diary and memoir, one night as I lay in bed, I felt a deep concern that my book might hurt or cause pain to my parents and family. But that night I had a vision dream. Both my parents came to me and showered me with love and forgiveness. It was a "feeling" dream more than "seeing," although I briefly saw both of their faces. I was then enveloped in a profound sense of forgiveness, flowing from me to them and reciprocated by each of them back to me. I then understood that I had their blessing with this memoir however flawed it may be.

To you the reader,

I hope you do not take this testimonial from my childhood as a prompt to conclude, "Huh, I get why she joined a cult." Because then you truly misunderstood me. My aim is to share my background to show where I came from. I am not saying that I have encountered the worst of the worst—I haven't, there's always worse in this world. But I want others to know that if you are considering a different way of life, you deserve it. I have been an imperfect child, friend, daughter, and sister. I have been an imperfect disciple. I have come from darkness. But I still found my way, with guidance and teachings of Maitreya. I want to tell you, reader, that if you doubt your worthiness of enlightenment through love, faith, and community, don't. Do not doubt yourself. Embrace where you have come from and let it propel you forward.

Do not let your self-doubt, which I have experienced, prevent you from reaching your own potential. We speak in this physical world about academic or professional potential, but what about spirituality? It is just as, if not more, important as those worldly accomplishments. Reader, you have the opportunity to gain experience and carry forth this universal truth. Do not take it lightly.
What if you met one of God's Awakened Ones of our Age in your own life? And yet you squandered this Gift?

Christians rail at this, but perhaps some will be open: What if you met "Jesus" (Yehoshua, later known as the Christ) in that lifetime he was here? But you failed and watched him suffer. You saw his sacrifices before your very eyes and yet you only reached a paltry few other souls with (Baptism, what have you)—we have the Gift of Holy Initiation and God's Promise. What would you do?

What do I do? Not enough. My usual present day-to-day is to keep a general spiritual Intention running in the background of every encounter, every conversation, every interaction of any kind with any living being (well, any being at all—living or recently deceased—I should say): *Please use me dear God, and dear Maitreya. Please work through me, around me, despite me, with me all there, or with me sometimes not all there—I ask to please extend Kijai, my intention of flowing the Power for Good that can do no wrong from Universal God and Maitreya, with harm to none and insofar as possible benefit to all. I surrender all my actions or inactions while accepting inescapable personal responsibility.* This has been my continuous personal prayer lately.

I went from that rocky family background into pure Spiritual Love and true Community of shared purpose. In short, Maitreya and everyone else who lived in the Ashram weren't just friends, we were a Spiritual Community. For the first time in my life, I truly felt like I was home. Unfortunately, I brought my own personal dysfunctional family habits with me.

Whenever the Community needed to teach me, by criticizing an action, I would take it as a complete rejection of me as an entire person. I could not see that the criticism was only of the specific behavior. Both parents partly rejected me when I was a child. So, criticism felt like an absolute rejection of my *entire* self. That is the absolute crux of it.

Yes, I forgive my parents and hope they forgive me too, but forgiving someone and recovering from the scars they left on you are two different things. I never felt like I fit in when I was growing up. I felt like I wasn't wanted, and no amount of forgiveness I came to extend for my parents could undo that. Being that isolated during such a formative time has lasting effects. One effect on me was that I never felt like I belonged anywhere. Not even with my family, my friends, or my husband.

A New Home—Mostly Squandered

That is why it meant so much to me when I first met Maitreya. The motivating factor was that I immediately found my purpose. This has not changed a bit to this very day. Our purpose will stand above and without regard to personality conflicts around it. But the involvement of being with others who clearly had similar spiritual experiences, even experiencing at the same time as me, and shared this same purpose, was and is a bond that will never fade.

Nobody made me feel more at home than Maitreya himself. We were a spiritual family; we did everything together. But every family has its ups and downs. I grew up with a host of anger issues, and because of that I had a host of regrets about how I interacted with those I care about, even those I love, and the Maitreyians were no exception.

I would often lash out if I felt we should be doing something differently than how things were being done. I often got into arguments with Maitreya himself about the best way to find more of our people who would accept Holy Initiation. We all know, don't we, that it is okay to disagree with someone, even a loved one, if you're respectful about it, but sometimes I'd lose my temper. I would start fights and I would belittle Maitreya, who was one of the most important people in the universe. I was rude to him, and that was not okay.

I felt guilty about some of the ways I had spoken to him, and the other members of the Community ever since to this day. I was stuck in Fight mode—and forced others to invoke the Flight mode. I switch to Fight at a moment's turn, and get stuck there.

Lighter Moments

It was not always hard with the Community either, we had lighter moments as well. We all enjoyed music. When we were all in Maitreya's van (as Shanti called it "Van-Go"), Maitreya would play many of his favorite songs and we often would sing along together. It might have been my imagination but as Simon and Garfunkel cried out lyrics of, *"Hear my words that I might teach you,"* Maitreya would look at me in the rearview mirror—as if talking to me about himself. And during the lines about, *"the boxer leaving and leaving but the fighter still remaining,"* he'd glance at me again—as if those words were about me.

Those road trips back in the late 1980's and through the 90's would often end in Westwood on the weekends. This was before cell phones and most computers. People were out on the street; many of them young people from UCLA. There was a corner we called "God Wars" where preachers would shout. Often Hare Krishnas would jump their dances of joy around the speakers. Maitreya would enthusiastically enter discussions with preachers and they always ended up as friends. This was especially true with one burly Hells Angels motorcyclist preacher who shouted at Maitreya in the beginning, but ended up hugging him by the end.

I remember one night in particular. It was not so peaceful for me that night. A preacher was yelling, "*Whore!*" at women walking by, including me, and I stopped and yelled at him. "*You don't even know who you are slandering. You don't know us!*" He grabbed my arm and twisted (causing what we called when we were kids, an "Indian Burn"). Once he let go of my arm, I ran up and related to Maitreya and the group what happened. Although they had not seen it, Maitreya told me to tell a police officer. When I told the nearby cops, they arrested me! The preacher had lied and said I assaulted him too. They arrested both myself and the preacher and I had to sit in a holding cell while The Friends went to an ATM and got my bail money. Months later we finally had a court date, and wouldn't you know it, that preacher didn't even show up. However, a nice Hare Krishna man who was my witness showed up on my behalf, which was so sweet of him to do so. He even submitted a written statement. I felt he was touched spiritually by Maitreya, as so many souls were. Charges were dropped from my so-called record.

In that same neighborhood and time, we did practice drills of "converge and disperse"—so much fun in Westwood. We walked in different directions from each other but then we would all arrive at another destination at the exact same moment. Maitreya also organized some protesters from Mandela City at UCLA—until he recognized that destructive communist elements were taking over.

As a Community, we also partook in a cultural phenomenon when Maitreya and all of joined in the "Hands Across America"— we all walked down to Pacific Coast Highway in May 1986 and held hands with strangers—a viral moment years before viral moments existed. Word went out on news and newspapers. We heard about it and joined in, almost like the modern-day flash mobs, suddenly appearing together and bringing momentary connectedness to everyone there.

Locally, in the 2000's, we hung out at several coffeehouses. Maitreya spoke for years about how coffeehouses were popular in the 60s, but there were none around us. Suddenly they became popular again. I believe he was putting that idea out in the zeitgeist. We frequented quite a few places in the South Bay, some of which are gone now.

We also often visited bookstores throughout the years. Back when I first came around, the traditional place was The Bodhi Tree in Los Angeles. It was a beautiful small new-age spiritual store, in two small buildings; one called the Annex was for used books. The main store was welcoming to seekers and readers. You could grab a cup of herbal tea for free and sit and read or talk to other seekers, which is what we often did. The best part is that the owner had hung up a magnificent 1978 photo of Maitreya up on the wall! It was right in line with other Awakened Ones' portraits displayed. I loved seeing that photo on their wall for years.

Since we were on the freeways a lot, Maitreya made his own bumper-stickers occasionally, with simple but profound messages on them. I loved those too. A few of my favorites were:

The Bitterest Truth is Far Sweeter Than the Sweetest Lie;

Fear is the Enemy—God is the Remedy;

God is Not a Christian;

God Created Evolution;

God is Not in Heaven—Heaven is in God;

A Closed Mind is a Very Dark Place;

A Man Searching For God is Like a Fish Searching for Water.

Maitreya had a quick sense of humor and his eyes would sparkle as he joked at times. But he told me once, something to the effect of, "*Don't let them know I joked. People like their spiritual founders to always be serious.*" But I will always remember his lightness along with the struggles. One such moment is the reason that I can never look at Night Blooming Jasmine plants without hearing Maitreya call it "Night Jamming Blues Men." Or silly things like calling dinnerware at the table "upsets" instead of "set ups." Or in-jokes, like saying "Spray here, as Psion would say," instead of "Stay here," because as you can guess, Psion the male cat was known for spraying his territory. Sometimes when I was too self-involved, Maitreya would tell me "*Egg-Bok,*" which we knew meant *Everything is Going to be OK.* Sometimes Maitreya would joke with me, that "just because you're paranoid doesn't mean they aren't really after you."

We had numerous Maitreya sayings that the Community will hold dear to our hearts forever.

I fondly recall a time when Maitreya joked with me although I thought he was being serious at first. He said "Repeat after me." And then "Om" "An" "Ahhh" "So" and then, "say that faster and faster." I stood there repeating each word and then all together faster. Then I stopped and laughed uproariously when I realized how it sounded like "I'm an asshole." He became red and I could see it went against his nature a bit, to poke fun at me like that. But he knew my personality and that I would laugh at it.

A sweeter notion he mentioned to me once was about the beauty of trees: "*Look at those trees, don't they seem like they are breathing?*" And so, they did. He knew the connectedness of all life and nature. We all witnessed numerous times his connection with animals—cats, dogs, squirrels, crows, all of life. We would see them communicate with each other—literally talking to each other. Some of these are on video—Maitreya and animals having a two-way conversation.

A little more on animals—Maitreya loved his cats. I was unfortunately allergic so it was one more obstacle for me while at their Center, Kaivalya Ashram. On one of our early days after I caused an emotional upset, his beautiful white fluffy kitty named Satwa sensed I was upset and came and sat in my lap, which never happened before or since that beautiful moment. We communed for a bit and I barely even sneezed.

Maitreya also unselfishly gave of his time and asked the Community to give their time for an assisted meditation at one point, to help me overcome the allergies. I vastly improved but still had mild issues afterwards. A harsh memory arose in the group meditation: I see my mom throwing a cat I had adopted across the kitchen floor. And then, the last memory of that cat I called Sneakers (it was black and white) haunted me a bit: my mom insisted that my brother take it to the woods and let it go. I never knew what happened to Sneakers. I was a senior in high school by then, but still considerably closed off emotionally, and not able to ask questions or deal with the situation. And so, a lingering slight allergy (which is sometimes tied with grief) remains perhaps along with a plain old physical disposition. But without that spiritual assistance it would most likely be much more pronounced.

Other Religions

Maitreya would often attempt to teach Christians that Jesus was not the only way, and that the word "only" was the "only" difference we had with them. Yes, Jesus will get you to Heaven. But then you will most likely need to come back. That one line in the Bible that I believe *should* have been taken literally is, "*Ye must be born again.*" And again, and again.

Arguing about reincarnation is like arguing with an atheist. What's the point? Sometimes Maitreya would shock a person with the comeback, "*God doesn't believe in you either,*" or "*I didn't believe in reincarnation last time I was here, either,*" just to wake them up a bit. Or, "*You can believe it's not raining out, but if you go outside in the rain, you'll still get wet.*" Belief is an okay starting place, but experience is the real teacher.

Maitreya also would expound a bit on how the Bible may have started as the Word of God, but was still of course written by man, through their own colored-lenses. And the famous Council of Nicaea occurred when rulers took out sections of the holy book that might raise people out of subjugation and believe they could be equals. Keeping the parts about bowing down before lords, I believe, is a reference to kings and governments, but that's just one take on it. Maitreya pointed out (what some scholars debated) that the passage about, "*Easier for a camel to go through the eye of a needle,*" was in fact a misprint. A little dot became missing over a letter—the word "rope" became "camel." You would have to admit, "Easier for a *rope* to go through the eye of a needle," makes a bit more sense, no? But those are just minor points.

The point—to Maitreyians—is that Maitreya wrote his own Holy Book, our Holy Book of Destiny. It was not dictated to someone else. It was not recorded years after he was gone. He wrote it himself. But even with our own book, Maitreya often drove-home the point that God cannot be contained in one small book. He would even toss it aside to make that point. Holy books are simply like fingers pointing toward the moon—the greater Universal Spirit. How could the immense God of All Creation be encompassed in one book? We always keep in mind that Letter without the Spirit is nothing, and words are just the Letter, you see. One of my favorite teachings from Maitreya is "the book of truth is within your own heart."

I was so honored to be in Maitreya's presence. When I first moved to L.A., it was thrilling to see Maitreya's childhood home, which he mentioned in his writings. I was honored to know Maitreya's family then, including his mom, Marian, who we visited on Sundays and took out to lunch. She was spunky and funny and believed in Maitreya, mainly because she had been a witness to his spiritual experiences as a boy. One time, she pointed at a classic painting of Jesus and said this was like her own son. She would turn red if one of us said she was not a virgin. Maitreya mentioned once that more than one religion insisted on a virgin birth. Again, the Enlightenment and Self-Realization had to be considered unobtainable by others; like the Bible being changed to keep people mostly subjugated. Not to say there are not beautiful parts of their book, the Psalms and Ecclesiastes among them. I never argue the bible with anyone. Why? It's theirs, not ours (although not rejected by us), and all True Founders of all True Religions were real and necessary.

We should all be getting along, not fighting amongst ourselves. If all the books were destroyed, it would not matter. Universal God is within the Hearts of All Souls. Maitreya taught that the Book of Truth is inscribed in every one of our own Hearts. Listen to that and read that, as I learned to do. I know it to be true that Universal God awakened within different men and women at different times for different reasons.

And, the big difference with The Friend's Way is that Maitreya was here Now, Presently, in our Lifetime. Turns out, most people prefer their spiritual founders to be dead, not looking right at them! As much as Christians may fantasize otherwise, if they had Jesus in their face for years, I would wager it would not be as blissful as they'd like to imagine. Don't you think? But it would be, as it was for myself in knowing Maitreya the Friend, an honor, a blessing, a miracle, a fight between bliss and despair that knows no bounds, and is only barely described here; a life to never forget and always treasure.

Maitreya mentioned how after he attained Oneness with Universal God the second time in 1977, he came back to the world in bliss and quickly found that he had to recreate his personality and ego. We cannot function in this material world without ego or personality. Also, as he said, *"Just because you become Enlightened, doesn't mean you can suddenly start playing the piano."* Meaning, you are not suddenly perfect in this world. All human beings are flawed; it is part of the lesson and experience of being here. Maitreya's personality could be described as: down-home corn-fed Iowan, with a humble, direct, clear matter-of-fact demeanor. He had a deep gentleness but could also be suddenly fierce in his passionate defense of the truth. He downplayed his high intelligence, but I found there was little he could not learn or do when he was determined to do so. He had a sweet sense of humor and would blush a little if jokes went a little overboard. He was not averse to righteous anger. He was patient with me, when I first arrived at his doorstep.

In the material world, I myself was inept at everything way back when I arrived at the Community. I could not fold my prayer shawl for the longest time. Tara, Maitreya's first disciple, would show me how to do it and I would just wind up getting frustrated. I'm not great at physical tasks, and she is. Tara's always been a hands-on person. She's a doer. She's the one that built the shrine in my apartment, including the banner, the wood planks, and the sitting bench. She even created beautiful paintings I have hanging up on my walls. I don't think she grasps how much it means to me that anyone would make something for me, and then gift those works to me; it really touches my heart. As much as I admired Tara, I never felt jealous of, or competitive, with her. I didn't need to. Maitreya did not play favorites; he was accepting of everybody—but protective of his Holy Cause above all else.

My most profound spiritual experiences with the Holy Community would happen when we practiced Inner Divine Communion together. We commune spiritually and sometimes have "Divine Speaking" that arise from Divine Revelations, shared with all. And, somehow shared for the first time within the speaker themself in that moment. Words and deep meaning come out, that were not even fully formed yet in consciousness. My mouth moves as my heart understands, all in the same moment—Divine Inspiration. One of them I exclaimed was, "Let Go—Let God," and somehow, I began hearing that in public later. Our zeitgeist is affected in ways I do not always understand.

We fervently shared experiences of Oneness with each other, with all Souls, with All Creation. We'd break through to the other side more times than can be recounted. We'd share our experiences with each other, as much as words could express such breakthroughs.

My Faith has shown our Bond will never be broken.

CHAPTER SEVEN

Many Gifts and Signs of Maitreya

Death doesn't scare me anymore. Neither did the passing of The Friend, Maitreya—it didn't scare me, but it did hurt me to the depths of my Being. However, I feared what would happen when Maitreya left this world. When we first got word that Maitreya's prostate cancer had returned, it was around 2005. The news hit me hard, and I could not stop crying. We were heading to dinner and I was riding in the back seat of the car. When we got to the restaurant, Maitreya told the others to head inside while he comforted me. That's exactly what he did. He got in the back seat where I was and just held me while I sobbed.

I could only focus on myself. I keep telling him, *"When you're gone, I won't be able to stay in the community."* He just gave me a slight sad, smile, and barely said a word. He knew I was being selfish, but he also understood. He knew his passing would be hard on all of us, and in a possibly unique way for myself, in certain isolating ways, because of the bumps we'd all experienced in our relationship.

What also bothers me about that day is that Maitreya then went on to give one of his most comprehensive talks ever during that dinner, and it did not occur to us to record it in any way. I had thought it would at least be accessible later because we were thinking of questions that might come up in a podcast, he was a guest on. All these years later, I can no longer find the podcast on the internet. It's gone. He gave a beautiful introductory talk about everything in his experiences and his religion. (There are hundreds of other talks, truly gifts, saved on tapes, CDs, YouTube, and other places like the Himalaya app.)

The doctors had given Maitreya only a few years around 2005 or so. He lived until 2012. He never appeared "sickly" at any time. He stuck to his routine of getting up and out amongst the people every single day until his final few days. Some rude people, more than one, have commented to the effect that, "*Maitreya should not have gotten cancer, and even if he did, he should have overcome it. A real spiritual person doesn't get cancer or succumb to it.*" This boils my blood over! How dare they say such a ridiculous idea? First, where is every single person who has ever previously been on earth? Dead, not here any longer. Second, and by God's Own Decree, Maitreya was an Ordinary Man with an Extraordinary Mission. He had to live as an ordinary mortal man. Ordinary people must suffer, get sick, and die in this world. There is no (physical) escape while in this world. And, ultimately, our entire religion is based on his two death experiences which were two Self-Sacrifices, his gifts to us. So, as you can see, he had already died twice before.

He was an ordinary man who took on extraordinary promises to God for the sake of others. And then at times, he was an extraordinary person stuck painfully in this ordinary and unknowing world. He came back here with The Friend's Way—of attaining True Enlightenment and Self-Realization, realizing by direct personal Experience that you are immortal and truly One with the One Universal God—so that we may all attain the Gift of Perfect Final Union with God, both within this life and at the end of it.

There is always an end to this life, no matter how much anyone may rail against that fact. Do I think he went too soon? Yes, of course. It is said that anything worth doing comes at a personal cost. But he paid too much. He paid with his life. I know that his premature death was partly due to stress. He had the unbearable stress of not fulfilling God's Promise of Divine Critical Mass while still in this earthly, a misunderstood existence. But he, and I, and all of us, die in this world at some point. I personally am flummoxed and a bit angry that people would demand otherwise. Yes, he has died to this world as we all will. But, the miracle is that Maitreya is now present in the hearts of all souls who call upon him. He is there! You will experience his presence in no uncertain way!

As in our Holy Book if Destiny: by the Will and Grace of the One Universal God: *"And you shall go about this world as an ordinary man struggling with all things with which ordinary men must struggle. And yet, within this ordinary man you shall be, verily, all of these things I have spoken unto you. And those who have eyes that cannot see beyond this ordinary shell and ears that cannot truly hear beyond this ordinary voice, will deny you and revile you. And this shall you endure for My sake. But those who have eyes that truly see, they shall see thee within an ordinary man and, verily, Me within thee. And those who have ears that truly hear, they shall hear The Truth even in thy most ordinary and mundane utterances and shall Know That I Am within you and your words."*

The Friend of All Souls, Maitreya. The Holy Book of Destiny (pp. 65-66). Kindle Edition.

Signs

I am fortunate I had, and still have to this day, so many Direct Personal Spiritual Experiences while still in this life. I had a myriad of shared experiences with the Spiritual Community, especially while we practiced Inner Divine Communion together. Maitreya also gave us signs of inspiration and guidance from beyond in the Spiritual Realm.

Maitreya had said shortly before he passed, *"Look for me in the clouds."* And sure enough, some of Maitreya's signs come in the form of clouds in the sky. These are worldly experiences that happen to me, while not even immersed in any meditative state.

Whenever I see one of Maitreya's signs, I like to document them: take photos of these clouds and such. It makes me feel closer to him, because I can still communicate with him. The clouds have been signs since Maitreya passed away from this world.

One such image that is special to me is when an angel appeared to me—a stereotypical looking angel in the clouds. I was in the old town section of Torrance sometime around 2014 or 2015 when I looked up in amazement and grabbed a photo on my phone.

And, in early April 2021, the very clear letters "G.O." appeared in clouds right over the room where I had just been meditating. This experience was mouth-droppingly incredulous. I had just asked if I should go to Florida to see my cousin who was battling cancer, and after I wrapped up my meditation, I went outside. I felt the urge to look up. When I did, I was rewarded by the letters "G" and "O" in the clouds right above the room where I had just meditated. It was the sort of perfect, straight-to-the-point sign I could expect from Maitreya — "*Go.*" Thank God and Maitreya, I did go. My cousin passed away a year later. She is in Heaven (I literally saw her happily there in several meditations). She did not accept Holy Initiation that I know of—yet. I expect she will need to come back to this world, but it is not really for me to know or say. Interestingly, her husband, who previously had zero spiritual experience or knowledge or interest, has now opened up to spiritual enlightenment. He has changed drastically since the time I asked Maitreya to help him in spirit, although he is just starting out and still learning meditation in general, not ours specifically.

More clouds. Recently in December 2021, a sideways question mark was in the clouds over my office. By the time I took a photo, the dot at the end of the question mark was floating away. To me, I took this as a sign from Maitreya asking me what I wanted. He had encouraged me get a great job at a wonderful law firm, but I still was not 100% happy. I complained and whined often because some of the tasks that both the attorneys—and Maitreya—had given me were sometimes difficult to learn.

As I thought about my complaining, and why I was being given the work, I had a thought: Perhaps all of this is to keep my brain sharp. I'd always worried about developing Alzheimer's disease. Sure enough, Irma, a masseuse friend of mine mentioned something out of the blue during one of our sessions. She said she thought Maitreya was taking care of me by helping me get a job that forces me to use my brain and keep it healthy. Funny that my complaints about my workload were explained to me and my thoughts validated by a friend who had no knowledge of what I had been thinking.

Shortly before publishing this memoir, another cloud appeared at the top of the back stairs I always climb to my apartment. I had been obsessing a bit while waiting for a medical test result. I wondered if I had cancer or something similarly serious. I looked up and saw what clearly looked like the profile of a head. I immediately laughed and said out loud, "Ok, Maitreya, I guess you're letting me know it's all in my head." And so it was, thankfully.

Maitreya's Material Creations

Truly, Maitreya the Friend of All Souls was and is the greatest man I ever knew and have known in my life. He was to me, one of the greatest men to ever walk this earth, and equally one of the greatest men in the Universe. Like most great men or women of this world, he went largely unnoticed spiritually, even though he was responsible for creating almost as much in the material world as the Spiritual Realm.

For example, he designed an all-metal Holy Book of Destiny which is held in The Smithsonian and Library of Congress since it is the world's only metal holy book. He also penned many books, leaflets, pamphlets, writings, plus many teachings and lectures, every day for years. He didn't use video much, until the 2000's. Although I wish there were more videos from the early days, there are some still on YouTube. He also produced electronic spiritual music and recorded them on CDs. He created spiritual hypnotherapy, including a sleep tape that I still, and often, use at night. (I started having insomnia in my late 40's and have it on-and-off to this day.)

There are some special videos and audio tapes we have where we are chanting together. It is a poignant moment for me to: sit in present time, and sing along with both my past self and Maitreya when past recordings were made. It is almost time-traveling. The juxtaposition of time periods overlapping is trippy to me.

Maitreya also recorded politically related talks and I helped mail those out to various talk show hosts, whose names I will not include for various reasons. We would hear his words and teachings being repeated back on a regular basis. He was reluctantly involved in politics when he saw how our society was going in a free fall in the wrong direction: away from Freedom and Responsibility, and toward Tyranny, Censorship, and complete lack of personal responsibility.

Otherwise, he reminded us that the only way to truly change the world is to change it spiritually. Once most people including politicians are truly spiritually enlightened, as to our true nature of Oneness and our highest attribute of Freedom, then that will affect everything else. Maitreya taught "Spiritual Evolution Within—for Political or Worldly Evolution outward". I've become an Independent voter and frankly have pulled away from the insanity of our times, unless I feel inspired on occasion to join in, with what I see as real Truth.

In Lomita, Maitreya also helped construct and build a deck at that house where he conducted meditations and sermons outside. Also in Lomita, he joined forces with the Baptist minister across the street to form a group which fought local crime.

Later in Redondo, he gathered people who helped build, after he envisioned it, an Empty Chair Memorial which became well known in the area. It is dedicated to all military service people of all branches, from all times. For years, he conducted ceremonies for the public at his Empty Chair Memorial in Redondo— as around 100 to 200 people would gather outside on Memorial Day weekend, and then also September 11th from 2003 to 2011. It is a well-known landmark in our town.

He created the Redondo Beach Memorial Day Parade where there was none before. He and Ila put an entire roster together for a wonderful event that the community enjoyed for several years. Shanti and Tara also tirelessly worked on many parade projects. I assisted Shanti with seeking out some donations. One year, I also helped track down local military heroes' families. It was beyond heart wrenching to connect with the families whose young men had given up their lives for their country. I was able to use my empathy for the good cause of connecting with those grieving families.

In honor of Memorial Day, Maitreya even arranged for a Navy Ship to visit Redondo Beach and ensured that they were welcomed in style. The Navy Captain told him it was one of the best portside visits they ever had.

He came up with the plans to improve and put in a Veterans Memorial at Redondo Beach Veterans Park—which at the time had next to nothing except a bit of a tattered flag. I witnessed him render the drawings on his computer for the plans for Veterans Park. I was then sitting at the meeting where the city people saw his rendering, and later stole it and claimed it as their own. They were not going to let him have credit for the history of improving Veterans Park. He would be too controversial of a figure for a City. He never did get his due credit, or as he called it, "*Just the truth.*"

And of course, since the beginning, he came up with the designs for our religion, inspired by Universal God. He created the Holy Shrine, the Sacred Scroll, a Mala, and other religious articles, for God's Eternal Universal Religion or Adhyatma-Yoga-Dharma, as The Friend's Way was also called. One of several favorites of mine is our Holy Pendant that we can wear, similar to a necklace. I especially liked having it made of wooden beads. But at one low point in the middle of a deserved criticism from the Community while in a restaurant, my pendant fell off and beads scattered all over the floor. My eyes started tearing up as I slowly crouched and picked up all the little beads under some questioning eyes of the servers. It felt symbolic: that I was causing destruction instead of progress.

The pendant came into material being when Maitreya had a vision dream years before I met him. He related how he saw himself in a forest and branches were across the path. He picked them up and made the "peace sign," but it was still missing something and he could not proceed. He then picked up another branch and solidly put it into place near the horizontal top of the peace sign and bam, he knew he made the symbol God wanted him to use. It is our sign of Victory—the inevitable triumph of Good over evil through God's Infinite Divine Grace.

These are all just outer representations of his teachings and an example of how he left a mark on the world both materially and spiritually.

Maitreya's physical life was a sacrifice. He gave up Perfect Union with God to come back to this world of suffering. He came back for each of us, not for himself. He could have stayed in Bliss—but he gave it up, for us. He came back for me. He came back for you. It is Maitreya's Self-Sacrifices that stand supreme beyond his material world sacrifices. His highest gift is from Universal God—the gift of true enlightenment and self-realization in this world and beyond it. For you. For me. For all of us, together.

Cloud—Archetypal Angel 2014—Torrance CA

Cloud—was a Question Mark above office 2021

My favorite Cloud photo—the Letters G.O., in 2021

All in My Head

CHAPTER EIGHT

~⋑

My Premonitions—
Early Spiritual Experiences

My Holy Initiation was my first purely spiritual experience, but that isn't to say I was a total skeptic before it happened. I had been exposed to the Spiritual Realm a bit before I became a Maitreyian.

Background

This may not be spiritual, but my basic foundation seems to be what is now called "highly sensitive." I remember as a child in school first hearing about chameleons that shift their appearance and colors according to their environment and absorb others, and thinking *"Oh, that's what I do!"* I have learned that children who grow up in chaos and trauma often become highly intuitive, because they learn they need to be on alert for the sake of their survival, to always be hyper-aware of their surroundings. Unfortunately, creating chaos also became part of the foundation of my personality, one that I am not proud nor happy about; in jobs, workplaces, relationships, friendships, and the spiritual community. Thankfully, I have improved in this pattern but I'm still working on it.

Being Sensitive in the Workplace

It is interesting to me that when compiling this memoir, all my many years of working in offices barely factor into what is important to me. But I am thankful God has always provided for me. And I like to think that my various office jobs held some sort of purpose of encountering, and perhaps transmitting Spiritual Contact to, so many different types of people. This "last" job I am at, happens to be with some exceptional people. It also factored into me taking so long to get this memoir completed, since I would only write on occasional weekends. Another lesson in Faith here: I found myself "in between" jobs a few times in my long life, and I never, not once, worried or lost faith. I always knew God would provide, and so it always came to be.

It is difficult for me to be in large groups of people, usually in offices; or other gatherings. I tend to pick up on what everybody is feeling. I can feel everyone's emotions, thoughts, actions, reactions, and what we call samskaras or unconscious patterns. But I do not always feel these things one-on-one (although often that is the case). Everybody's thoughts and energies sometimes all mix into one big, pea soup. The result is at times a constant low buzz around me any-where I go, wherever there are people and emotions to pick up on. It's exhausting. Whenever I'm stressed, or I'm not sleeping enough (which is often), I get more vulnerable to this big static pea soup and the buzzing gets louder. I also usually cannot abide watching violence on TV shows or movies; frankly, I don't understand murder being entertainment. These days, people would call this personality type or phenomenon, "being an empath" which for some reason is fashionable now in our zeitgeist. I often just call it a burden.

I will never be the kind of person whose eulogy at a memorial includes phrases like, "When she walked into a room, the room got brighter," along with the usual comments about "great energy." The truth is, my energy often became chaotic, sometimes complicated by my late-onset insomnia. More often than not, this chaos stemmed from picking up on the thoughts, fears, and assumptions of those around me, leading me to feel overwhelmed in a "feeling" avalanche or fog.

It is not just the regular work stress that would get to me: it was the additional underlying aspect of me "not doing my real job in the world"—the ongoing turmoil in my soul that I was not fulfilling my vows to God and Maitreya. My poor unsuspecting employers probably think I'm a complete basket case at this point—they may well be correct. Perhaps I *should* be frantic and out-of-sorts, considering I had such an important Spiritual Cause that I was not advancing in the world. As Maitreya used to say in the beginning, "*Go about this work as if your hair were on fire and you were looking for water.*" He would point out, that if we truly grasped it all, that is how our attitudes would be.

Premonitions

I did experience what some might call psychic experiences and premonitions throughout my life. To be clear, our religion is not about being psychic. Maitreya made it a point that it is important not to get lost or stuck on that path. It's an interesting phenomenon some of us experience. I do not want it to be a diversion from the bigger Holy Cause. It just happens to be a part of my life experience, for years since I was a child. Also, I am not proclaiming myself as an actual psychic, especially not one who could or would ever read for others. These are my own experiences, alone, and part of the fabric of my worldly being, some before I joined the spiritual community. We also like to make it clear that "no one is a channel," as no one speaks "for" Maitreya. Anyone can call on him in their hearts and communicate with him and God themselves. We can all have Faith through Experience.

Earlier Premonitions and Experiences

The earliest spiritual-type experience I can remember was when I was around two or three years old, maybe younger. I believe I was in the backward-facing back seat of my parents' station wagon (I'm also told it might have been a VW van) when suddenly, that large back door swung open and I spilled out onto the highway. I'm also told there was a silence at first, followed by my mom yelling, "*The baby!*" My recollection is blurry, but I do remember laying on asphalt when a male voice urgently yelled at me to, "*Get up! Get up!*" I looked up to see an older man wearing a dark suit and hat who was yelling at me to hurry up and move. I got up and ran towards my parents, who were by then parked on the side of the road. As I ran towards them, I was giggling because I thought it was fun. Another driver, a man in the car behind us, almost ran me over, because he thought I was a doll when other toys fell out with me. He didn't realize I was a kid until I got up and started moving, just like that mysterious old man prompted me to do. I never figured out who or what that spirit was that came up to me and told me to move so I wouldn't get run over, but it's thanks to that divine intervention that I'm still here today.

I had a vivid Vision Dream when I was a kid. I was about 10 years old in the early 70's. I woke up, rewinding it in detail, although now I remember only parts of it. I was watching future society like an observer, and I was amazed at what I saw. I saw people buying new clothes that had rips in them on purpose, men who said they were women, and women who said they were men—with not just sexual preference, but an actual mixed-up identity in the world. I saw a curious zeitgeist of people preferring lies to truth, songs that became so simple they were almost gibberish, and most of all I saw nuclear bombs hitting earth while I just walked on a beach. Quite a dream. My gut feeling is that the last part is a metaphor—I hope. It was perhaps more of a message: to do what we need to do now with Maitreya's Mission, so that we do Not have nuclear war!

Other unusual childhood experiences also stand out. When I was a pre-teen, I was invited to my neighbor's party across the street. I think they are Lebanese. As I entered their house, I clearly saw a group of women in full black dresses with black veils on, lined up together on a couch. I started to ask my neighbor friend who they were, but suddenly they weren't there anymore; the couch was empty.

As shaken up as I was, I knew to keep my mouth shut. For some reason, I proceeded to eat as if I was starving. I gorged on peanut butter and jelly sandwiches and cake outside, while refusing to go back into that living room again.

During these teenage years, I also asked God how long I would live. I asked Him what year I would die. Just like that, a year started coming to me. I changed my mind and asked God to stop at the last minute, but I did hear and see the first two numbers— "2" and "0". This sounds obvious now, but this was decades ago, and it was because of this chat with God that I always knew I would at least make it through the 1990s.

I don't know if it was the same guardian angel I'd come across when I was a kid, or Maitreya himself who I was destined to meet, but throughout my teenage years I also occasionally heard a deep melodic male voice telling me, "*This too shall pass,*" exactly when I needed to hear it—more than once.

There were so many flashes of insights over the years. During one of my first bank jobs when younger, my friend and coworker Betty hadn't arrived yet. I felt a gentle voice calmly tell me, "*She was in an accident but she's ok.*" Not a minute later, I took a call from a relative of hers—saying the exact same words.

In the early 1980's, I had the premonition that I was about to meet my husband. I distinctly remember being in the funky old San Francisco bathroom in my friend Shanti's and my apartment, getting ready to go out, and a sudden complete knowingness came upon me: *You are going to meet your husband tonight.* We met while Shanti and I were at a bus stop. Rich and his brother drove up to the curb in a truck and asked if we wanted a ride. We fatefully got in. As I sat next to him, I immediately *knew* him. It is possible we knew each other in past lives. We proceeded to laugh and joke all through the night. It had been raining so we later determined that our song could be "Bus Stop," waiting in the rain at the stop, sharing an umbrella, and meeting for the first time, leading to a vow of a long relationship.

More recently, we had a local incident around 2015, when there was a terrible car crash down the street near a church. I walked by the area a day or two later and strongly smelled the scent of perfume. I looked all over and found zero bottles. One of the women who died in the accident was older, and I felt like it was her presence that gave me the scent of perfume. So, I helped her find Maitreya and the spiritual realm, even after she had passed on from this world.

I had a prior premonition with another elderly woman, and luckily this did not turn out to be tragic, although I once again did not take the right action. I was a volunteer and would go food shopping for her. One day, I kept thinking about her over and over, to the point I envisioned going to her assisted living center to make sure that she was okay. But I didn't do it. The next time I met with her, she said the exact day that I had those feelings she had fallen in the bathroom, could not get up and couldn't reach the phone. She said she purposely sent me telepathic messages—since we had talked a little about such things. Luckily for her, someone in the center finally checked on her. She spent hours on the floor and had desperately tried to let me know. She succeeded, but I had talked myself out of taking any action.

A sweeter experience occurred recently, around April 2022. I clearly saw a friend very much looking pregnant before she had told anyone. Elena also happens to be Russian and a wonderful health-worker currently working in cranio-sacral therapy. I always called on Maitreya to be present in our sessions, and the subsequent experiences and visions did not disappoint. One day I envisioned her standing at the massage table, very pregnant. It was just a flash of her, standing there looking maybe six months along. I waited until we were done and then said *"Um, I'm not sure how you'll react to this, but I just saw clearly that you were standing here pregnant."* She was shocked and said, *"Shraddha, I just found out a few days ago—and only my husband and I know about it."* She later invited me to her baby shower.

I had another experience after one of our sessions. I was hugging her goodbye and suddenly felt strange words tumble out of my mouth. She pulled back in amazement and exclaimed, *"You know Russian?"* Of course, I do not and she had to tell me, *"You just said 'thank you,' in Russian."* I exclaimed, *"I think that was Maitreya!"* It sounded like "Spa-See-Bough." This was a very cool experience! A modern-day "speaking-in-tongues" in a language I did not actually know, and did not think about, before the words came rushing out.

Family Premonitions / Life Assistance Meditations with Maitreya the Friend

There have been other more recent premonitions, including warnings to both the suicides in our family. I felt a strong urge to finally join Facebook out of the concern that something might happen to a niece or nephew. Shortly after I joined, my nephew posted "It's better this way." Unfortunately, I did not take it as seriously as I should have. Being new to it all, when his friends "liked" it, I thought it was just some random comment they all understood. He killed himself soon after that post. I wish I had done more. Then only a few years later, out of nowhere, I had a strong impulse to visit my older nephew in Colorado. I kept making draft itineraries in Expedia and saving them and planning when I would go. But then his step-son shot himself. Why did I have a strong urge to go there right before it happened? Could I have helped prevent both these tragedies? I don't think so. But it is deeply haunting.

At least I was able to give Life Assistance as Maitreya taught us and I helped guide a few souls to Maitreya in the Spiritual Realm.

Recently in August 2022, after a niece gave the sad news that her ex-husband died of a drug overdose (apparently after years of an on-and-off OxyContin addiction), I did a nightly meditation and prayer for two nights. The next night, I had a powerful encounter during meditation. I realized I needed to once again do our full Life Assistance.

I set myself aside, and connected and communed spiritually with this former nephew-in-law. I asked if he accepted spiritual assistance, and he said yes. I introduced him in the spiritual realm to Maitreya, The Friend of All Souls. I don't always receive visual or audio type experiences, except for a bit. I usually get almost overwhelmed with just the feelings' part. This time I had *all* of it including visuals, and overall, everything felt beautifully touching.

Todd was clearly standing there with tears running down his face. The feelings were of intense sadness. He was asking—begging—for forgiveness. Maitreya walked up to him in his full yellow shawl and yellow clothes he would wear for our Sanctuary meditations. They turned to face each other. I was seeing this as if I was looking at them and they were sideways, looking at each other. Todd was still crying as Maitreya walked over and I saw, felt, knew, a big hug sent and received. I heard Maitreya say, "*Welcome Brother.*" Todd was still asking for forgiveness, almost non-stop. Then, a lot of Light and Love and Peacefulness, but not complete peace yet. It is hard to explain, there was a piercing sadness accompanied by beauty.

I questioned for a second, as I sometimes do, to kind of check-in and make sure this was a spiritual vision and not just my own mental imaginings or imagination. (Although it was a very clear event.) Maitreya turned and faced me. He gave me a slow, both-eyes blink, with a slight closed-lip smile; this is something he would do while in this material world. It is his Reassuring look. Very gently closing and opening of both eyes. Then he turned back to keep hugging Todd. There was still sadness mixed with peace as I pulled back from the experience.

I called my sister, Todd's former mother-in-law, and when we had our phone call, there was interference on the line. I think that interference was just him saying hello.

I do expect more peace to be on the way, but he might have some more work to do to get there. That is why it's so beautiful to me that he accepted spiritual assistance. I knew he had accepted Holy

Initiation, and Maitreya is now at his side for every second onward. It has little to do with me personally. I just direct the assistance and try to help arrange the exceptional meeting with willing Souls. This nephew wasn't concerned with *me*; he was concerned with his soul's well-being and the forgiveness of every member of his close family. Now he was no longer alone spiritually. The Friend of All Souls was clearly right in front of me, with him.

We have other drug and alcohol addictions in the family. I Flow the Power for Good to them all the time. Two of my nieces also got into heroin—this is the society we are in now. One niece has recovered and is helping others. I really poured forth all the spiritual assistance I could over many years, and I think she was receptive. But another niece was still deeply entrenched in drug use. One brother is doing great with no more drinking, but another not-as-much, and yet better; and yet another nephew is currently in rehab. I know God and The Friend help them as much as possible. It always comes down to one's Free Will, always, but easier to say than live by those consequences.

One More Life Assistance

An unfortunate update, but my niece, Claire, lost her battle with addiction in October 2023. This time fentanyl was involved. We had several spiritual communications over a few days. At first, I only felt a sad connection, but did hear, "Grandpa" which I took to mean my Dad, her grandfather, was with her. After a few attempts where not much happened, I was inspired to tell Claire, *"I'm not asking you to Believe, I'm asking if you accept Spiritual Assistance of your own free will."* And then, boom, there she was. I had my eyes closed but could see her in my mind's eye, sitting across from me. I could feel her thin wrists when I took them to Extend and Flow the Power for Good that can do no wrong (Maitreya's Kijai). She accepted the assistance and I felt peace wash over both of us. I called her mother afterwards and as I was saying *"I'm not done yet, though,"* I briefly felt and clearly heard Claire laugh a bit. As I mentioned this laughter, both my sister and I got the chills up and down our arms with the hairs standing up, as happens when I know Spirit is right there. I had some more experiences the next few days: I saw her sitting at a desk in a class-room and I knew she was telling me she was busy learning lessons. I felt her life here was to learn lessons, and as soon as she passed, she was learning more Spiritual lessons. I knew that she enjoyed and appreciated this learning in the spiritual realm. There was absolutely some peace, but not total complete peace; that is just my experience with her at this point.

My sister also finally got the sign she was begging Claire for. While driving Claire's ashes to the funeral home, her radio—which was always tuned into a type of (I think) country rock station—suddenly played Cold Play's "Fix You," a song with deep meaning. (I'm told they would argue—my sister declaring, "*That song is about me trying to fix you,*" and Claire retorting, "*I don't need to be fixed.*") Then, it went on to play the songs that were to be in the background at the memorial, one after another, even when in the usual dead zones where her radio never worked. Not coincidences, don't you think?

Generally, sometimes I have goosebumps when talking about a loved one who passed. I know that means they are with us at that moment. When I was at one of my nephew's weddings in New York, I mentioned how my Dad lamented that one of his regrets about dying was not knowing what would become of his grandchildren, especially this particular nephew. We both got goosebumps when I was relating this memory, and we agreed it was a sign from Dad/ his Grandfather at that moment.

More Premonitions

Some of these are on a bigger scale (not just my immediate sur-roundings):

More historically, in 2000, I had plans to fly to the East Coast with my then-boyfriend, and decided to meditate and ask if we were going to be safe. I had at least two visions that came to me, both showing me the same grim future: planes flying into tall buildings in New York. When the Maitreyians asked me if I did a Circle of White Light of Protection before our trip, I told them what I had vividly saw, and they stared at me in a bit of confusion. I told them that I firmly knew that the planes I saw crash into buildings in New York were not the planes I was scheduled to fly on, and the attack was not going to be that year. Once there, I also had feelings of dread while looking at postcards and t-shirts of the World Trade Center and I kept telling my boyfriend, *I don't want to look at those. I only want to look at the Statue of Liberty cards and shirts, not the World Trade Center.* Weird, huh? Of course, I recalled all this the next year, on the awful day of September 11, 2001. I had also had foreboding feelings whenever I saw "911" whether it was the emergency number or a date, for many years preceding the fateful day.

A much earlier but related premonition of September 11, 2001, came to me when I was a young teenager visiting the World Trade Center a few years after it had opened in the mid-1970s. My Aunt Dot took a few of us to visit. I remember stepping off the elevator into a restaurant and being completely terrified. I heard a male voice declare with certainty, *"They're all going to die."* I had no idea why or when. (Or why the premonition wasn't time-specific.) I refused to look at the views of the city from above, as my knees shook the entire time. I begged to go back down and never told anyone what I heard. The deep sadness mixed with terror was too much for me to contemplate. I shoved the feelings down. They would only surface a few more times over the years.

Another cultural premonition occurred when the news amplified, and most people worried about "Y2K," when it became the year 2000, simply because computers were mis-programmed, and anticipated there would be some kind of catastrophe upon us on January 1. I laughed and was certain nothing would happen, and so it was. Although if I had been wrong, I suppose I would just not mention it. It's said that hard work from programmers prevented a catastrophe from the first oversight.

Around 2003, I related to Maitreya that I had asked God where Saddam Hussein was, and felt the answer was "underground" and "close by" where they were searching for him. Maitreya suggested I put this in a letter and mail it to myself to show the postmark. This of course was an excellent idea. Unfortunately, I got caught up in our everyday life and did not follow through, a procrastination consistent with my personality flaws.

Reincarnation

I also had, like many do to some degree, a sense of my past lives. These past lives never presented themselves to me as more than a distant, fuzzy memory, but I was certain that I had lived them. I've always felt an affinity for being Jewish. Specifically, I believe I was alive during Jesus's time. And, I think I was also alive during the Holocaust. Another is that I always felt a rapport with Japanese lifestyles. I never quite got the specifics, because my mind is much more focused on the life I am currently living, but I know these previous lives happened. They all have ripples that I can still feel to this day. I do remember being around 14 and my Dad talking at the dinner table about his Army experiences. He recounted his troop liberating a French village and finding Nazi paraphernalia. I felt a shock run through me. I exclaimed *"The Nazis were in your lifetime? That was only around 30 years ago?"* I truly thought the evil era of Nazis had occurred lifetimes ago. I felt a deep disappointment at how unevolved humanity still was, which of course was an odd reaction from a kid. My first memory was before I was born; my mother was giving birth and I heard her say to someone, perhaps a doctor, "Yeah, Right" in a disgusted tone.

I had memories that in a previous life I was hanged, and now I still have neck problems, even in a completely new body. Yes, neck problems. Perhaps this is because my soul is still processing what happened to it.

Whenever people say, *"You only live once,"* I just laugh. We have all been here many times, but the goal is to get off this Wheel of

Birth and Death and go all the way home to Oneness with Universal God.

Occasionally, when I meet someone new, I can tell that we knew each other in a past life. Shanti was one of those people. I would actively have to remind myself, *Oh, that's right. She's different in this lifetime.* These are my feelings; I can't speak for the truth of her own different lifetimes. We cannot speak for each other, only for ourselves.

A few years ago in a previous employment, one of my bosses who I tend to get along with, came to me in a dream and showed me how we had known each other in a past life. In the dream, we were working on a project together and planning some kind of engineering or construction type job. It was quite vivid, but strange. I never mentioned it to them, but it did explain our slight connection and respect for each other, no matter what.

When I was a teenager, I woke up in a panic because my husband wasn't next to me and then wondered where my children were. I was gripped by at least five minutes of panic and tearful grief because they weren't there. I finally came to the present moment and knew I had been immersed in a different lifetime—with a vision that stayed with me until this day, although I never mentioned it to anyone.

A somewhat fascinating observation I (and other reincarnation theorists) notice: some of us have birth marks that could possibly be connected to past lives. I feel that the large birth mark in the middle of my back looks like it could have been a bullet or other weapon killing me in one lifetime (perhaps stabbed in the back) -- but as usual details of other lives are fuzzy.

Another phenomenon sounds odd but: as I work in law offices, whenever I see the word "executed" my heart skips a beat. Instead of barely registering that it's just "signing" a document, I instead have a whole-body memory of being executed for my beliefs. I try not to dwell on that though.

Life Assistance

The meditation we would only occasionally perform together as a community, and which I practiced by myself (as mentioned here earlier) using Maitreya's teachings and in his Holy Book of Destiny, is called the "Life Assistance Meditation." I also practiced it with people who just passed from this earth. This is not a psychic exercise, this is a true Spiritual Principle and tool that Maitreya gave us, that any Maitreyian can perform whether they had past experiences or not. It is a way Maitreya gives to truly Commune with a Soul, Spirit-to-Spirit, so as to assist them.

The first time we did this, it was for a high-spirited beautiful young waitress from the Swedish Corner smorgasbord who died tragically in a car crash in 1987. She was still in a coma and we all felt like she was hanging on for her family but really wanted to leave. She didn't feel her body was something she could come back to, and at the same time she wanted to move on to something indescribably beautiful. So, we helped guide her towards Maitreya in the spiritual realm, in hopes of helping her reach the interconnected oneness with all that awaits anyone who will accept Holy Initiation.

More recently, something similar to my family incidents happened around Christmas in 2021 (still "Covid" days) that made me, once again, reevaluate how I see death and the immortality of the Soul. I was sitting on my couch, on an early Tuesday evening, and clearly heard a gunshot ring out from the quiet, cold stillness. I immediately suspected what the sound was. It wasn't a car backfiring or a firework shooting off. The gunshot sounded so close and loud. Following long moments of silence, I began to hear the sirens getting closer. I was used to hearing sirens because I live near a police station, so I didn't go outside to look. It was days later that I learned the source of that single gunshot. Tragically, a 12-year-old boy took his own life. This family lives only four houses away from me.

At first, I just extended Maitreya's Kijai (Flowed the Power for Good that can do No Wrong) to the boy, but I couldn't fully concentrate.

A day later, I was looking at the clouds through the back window of my apartment and wondered, *Does that look like the letters IDC?* It did. This was the Universe reminding me to do Inner Divine Communion for Levi, because I had not done enough yet. (I forgot to take a photo of those clouds.) I gave in and connected with him in Life Assistance. Even though this poor boy was deceased, I still of course felt a connection with him. I repeated *"It is done, you can't go back and change it, you must keep going. Maitreya the Friend of All Souls will help you, let him help you."* I know I asked God and Maitreya to assist him in our spiritual meditation. In fact, the same way I had helped my nephews who had also taken themselves away too soon. It's so sad, but also bittersweet because these young boys were all rescued by Maitreya in the Spiritual Realm.

Years ago, as a Community we also did a Spiritual Assistance meditation as a favor for a coworker of mine who lost her newborn baby and who was incredibly distraught. Bernadette's connection to her baby's spirit was strong. He thanked her for giving him a chance to briefly walk among us, and allow him time to atone for karma he'd accrued from another life. Bernadette didn't like that, but I could only tell her the truth of the experience.

This reluctance of the receiver, is reminiscent of the time in the late 90's when I visited my brother and his wife, who I sometimes had tense issues with. Maitreya told me, in person not just in spirit, to *"Just keep praying for them the whole time you are there, keep Flowing the Power for Good that Can do No Wrong."* So, I sat in their backyard in rural Pennsylvania during that visit, and just kept Flowing the Power for Good from God and Maitreya to them. Shortly after, my brother's wife found out she was pregnant with her "miracle baby." My sister-in-law partly attributed this to the Virgin Mary statue she buried in that same yard. Who am I to say for certain? But I know what I did, or more accurately, what I had asked Universal God and Maitreya to do, and I have always been happy for all of them, no matter what personality issues would arise over the years.

On that brief topic of Christianity again, I wish I could share my knowledge of Jesus with my Christian relatives and friends. But I'll share it with you here. I had an unforgettable waking-vision one day in the early 1990's when I was working a temporary job at a construction office in Hollywood. A muscular, swarthy middle eastern, man in his 30's in a t-shirt and with a slight beard, walked in and I suddenly thought with a recognition, "*wow, he looks just like Yeshua (Jesus) looked when he was here.*" I will never forget that startling moment.

It harkened back to a childhood experience I had. When I was a young girl in Catholic School, while the nun was droning on something about Jesus, I clearly heard the words, "*My name was Yeshua.*" (This sounded like Yo-ho-shu-way"). This popped into my mind, in a beautiful strong melodic male voice. Now I reply, "*My name is Shraddha—which is Faith in you and all of God's Awakened ones of all time, but especially as a follower of Maitreya the Friend of All Souls.*"

Heaven and Hell

While there might not exactly be a Heaven or Hell sort of afterlife that is permanent like Christianity teaches (although that is partly true), the Soul is immortal and part of the one Universe, both manifest and unmanifest.

As Maitreya taught from his own experience, Hell is that time after leaving the body where the Soul must experience all the wrong it caused in this world, a "burning off." Heaven is that time and place in consciousness where the Soul is able to enjoy all the good caused in the world, and also rest easy in comfort with their previously deceased relatives if still in the spiritual realm.

But, then each Soul must go on. Either go back to this world of life, suffering, sorrow, old age, illness, and death, on the endless Wheel (as we call it). Or, be set free from the Wheel, to go Home to Perfect Final Union with the One Universal God, as a drop of water returns to the Sea from which it has come, and to which it will return.

Maitreya came back to give us a way to get all the way Home. There is no more reason to fear death. No matter how primal the fear is to the physical body, we as pure Spirit have no need to fear it.

I know with absolute certainty when I am spiritually communicating with someone, just as surely and as easily as anyone knows when they just had a regular conversation with someone in the material world. They, of course, know it happened and it is not just in their mind. Do you know when you just had a conversation with someone? Of course.

Maitreya used to say his spiritual certainty was like, "*I know it, like I know I got out of bed this morning. Nothing to really argue about.*" Sometimes, I feel this knowingness is the same as the faith in the sun. I know it will go down at night and come up in the morning and I never need to question it. That is an example of how much my Faith in Maitreya became a part of the fabric of my very being.

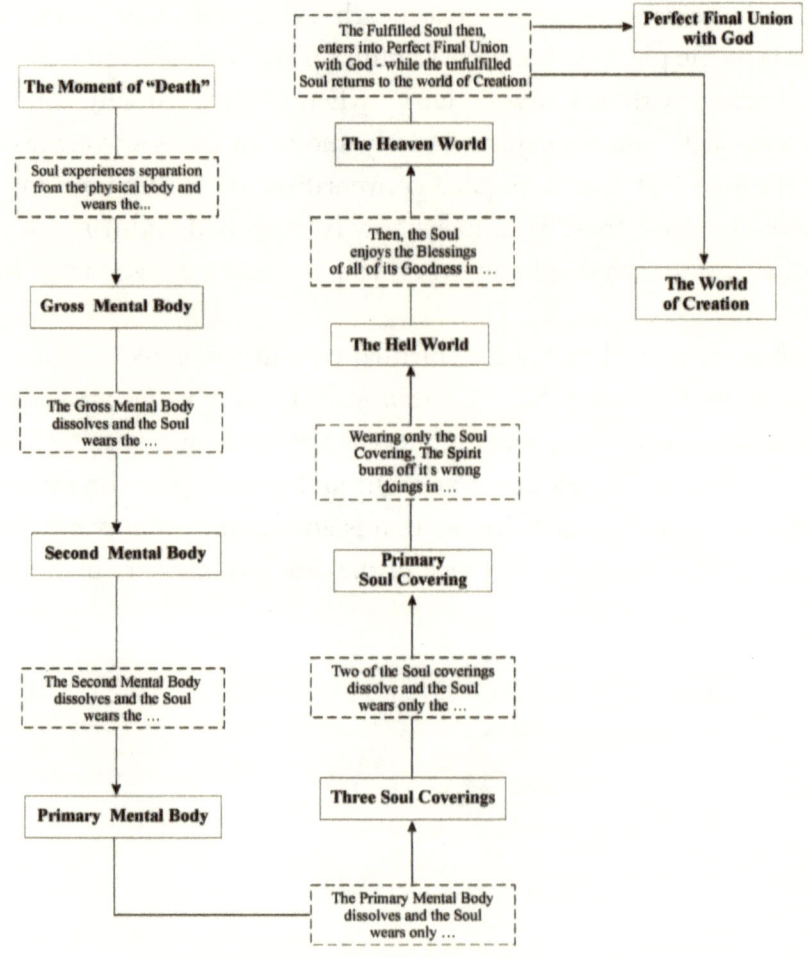

What Happens When We Die

Maitreya Bhagavan The Friend

～⊃

CHAPTER NINE

The Friends

Worldly Friends

L et me start with this: sometimes it felt like God also put friends in my material world so they would be there for me when I needed them and I wouldn't be alone in this world. I was never alone spiritually, but my other friends helped me navigate the material world. My friend, Michelle A., is one of those. Her husband is also a friend and like a brother to me even though I don't see them often. She received Holy Initiation but did not wish to become a full community member. (One reason might be her being forced into Jehovah's Witness as a child, I don't know). However, she works on perfecting her Enlightenment to this day. Unfortunately, as happens with others sometimes, when she has clear spiritual experiences of Maitreya, and after having received the Friend's Holy Initiation of True Enlightenment, she does not always attribute them to that fact. There is not a lot I can do about that.

I've known her so long, that I remember around 1991 or so, I didn't know the meaning of "www", or much about the internet, and she was the one who told me. A slight detour on this topic of computers: this reminds me how, around 2005 or so, Maitreya was in front of his computer, as he usually was, and I asked Maitreya and

Ila why they didn't just "Google" something. They both kept asking, "What?" They thought I was saying gibberish when I kept repeating, "*Google it!*" I also smile when I remember Maitreya later saying that "LOL" should mean Lots of Love. (Everyone then glanced at me, maybe thinking I'd say something corrective or snide about it; but I said, in all honesty, that was the sweetest thought—what a better world it would be if that's what LOL meant). My first email address was *somthg2say*, because I wanted to get the word out about Maitreya. Turns out, I did not say enough over the years.

Maitreya was more into technology than I was. He bought one of the first home personal computers on the market. Maitreya was also the one who showed me the first cell phone I ever held. He also was the first person I ever saw receive Amazon packages, which he excitedly opened. He was immediately into almost all technology when it came out.

It is interesting that our religion began before the internet and even home computers. But once the technological revolution occurred, Maitreya immediately learned and used all methods of communication with people as soon as they were available.

Point also being, sometimes it's hard to believe how many years have gone by with the world changing so swiftly in the material and tech world and yet changing so slowly from the spiritual perspective. We have so far to go in this world as people search for more than materialism.

My other worldly friends included Dee (also Initiated but not wanting more at this point); Cassie, my friend and neighbor; Irma who is both a spiritual sister and a friend and a gifted healer (her bond with Maitreya is quite strong); Elena (now in Florida), similar to Irma as I consider her a type of spiritual sister and healer; Julie, who I've known for over 30 years; Tom (also accepted Initiation but did not progress much; but was an ex-boyfriend who remains a friend); and another Michelle, who lives nearby and is a beautiful soul—and like others who always stepped in right when I needed them and I will be forever grateful.

I did have a few "normal" relationships. My marriage was typically sweet and non-violent except for one mild fight when he was drinking. I had several meaningful relationships in later years but unfortunately, they didn't work out either. One nice guy named Mike received Holy Initiation and had study meetings with Maitreya, but he seemed to stay stuck in his same patterns and not progress. I probably didn't help him much—my hormones were out of whack and I nagged him almost constantly, to my forever embarrassment. (I thank God I later outgrew that "nagging" pattern.) Mike had two children and I was able to have a good influence on them. Kristy and Kyle also had the honor of meeting Maitreya, although they were so young I don't know how much they remember at this time, but I know they were blessed. I tried to remain friends with Mike but lost track of him; he is not on social media.

Dee is also a wonderful soul. We are able to talk freely even when we need to ramble about our stressful law office jobs. She even experienced seeing Maitreya put his arms through hers, to guide her through an intention on changing her employment situation. She related this nonchalantly (which others have also done over the years). I think friends who have reported these spiritual experiences are afraid I'll push them, so they just act like it's a natural occurrence to experience seeing, envisioning, and feeling Maitreya right there in front of them!

There really is no need to push—either someone is calling on Maitreya the Friend in their own hearts or they are not. It is between them, God, and Maitreya.

I needed these worldly friends (even some on Facebook) when I would cause issues and disharmony in my Spiritual Community who would then need to distance themselves from me at times. I would be able to then turn to worldly friends, because God let me know I am never alone. But it could be difficult "out in the world"—as I would yearn for the commonality and shared spiritual experiences with my true Spiritual Community. The bond with them is like no other.

Of course, since the instant of the Bond of Holy Initiation, I literally was never Spiritually alone again. Maitreya has always been with me in Spirit from that moment on, forever. This bond stands supreme above all others.

The Friends—Spiritual Friends and Followers of Maitreya The Friend of All Souls

In my mind, Shanti is a treasure. *All* Maitreyians are treasures. But we do have a bond that is special to me (more special to me than to her or others): she is also my Spiritual Guardian. Unfortunately, I do not have as much time with her now as I would like, especially as time flies by, but I value every minute together that we do have. Shanti has a heart of gold and an incredibly inquisitive mind. I will walk away after a conversation with her and realize she asked me all the questions, but I didn't ask many of her. She has a genuine sincere interest in every person she meets. She can be a real social connector, which I view as a gift that I don't particularly share. She has that boundless faith in Maitreya that will never be shaken.

My initial impression of our first leader, Tara, was how soft her big, beautiful eyes were. She can look right through to my spirit, while being both gentle and stern—an elder who always has something to teach me. She has a melodic tone in her voice that is always pleasing to hear, no matter what else might be going on around, or within, me. She was one of Maitreya's first disciples, who took that leap of faith that not many could or would do. And she is one of the only original followers to have stayed to this very day. She knew Bhagavan before his second self-realization. After he related that experience in 1977, she told others who doubted him, "*I know him. I believe him.*" She became the first disciple.

I sometimes see myself as the Bad Disciple. Although of course I wasn't entirely bad. A bad disciple at times, but always and forever a faithful believer.

Ila is bold and forthright in her upholding of the purity of our religion that is entrusted to her and all of us. Her insights sometimes catch me by surprise, in the way flashes of understanding can burst through whatever chatter is in my mind, because she is so on-point.

Ila had arrived at the Ashram a few years after me, with her husband at the time, Sean. I believe I helped give her Maitreya's initial Spiritual Contact. Our spiritual brother Satya and I were driving in his VW van and saw this cool young hippie couple on a motorcycle. I exclaimed, "We have to give them a flyer!" and Satya followed them until we could get alongside. Finally, we were stopped side-by-side at a red light, and Satya leaned over and handed Sean a flyer to a "Love-In" that Maitreya was leading in Griffith Park at the time. Ila and Sean were living in an RV and Ila was teaching kids at the YMCA. I encouraged her to get a job as a legal assistant like the rest of us, gave a great reference (which she deserved); and she stayed with associated attorneys for many years. Ila was shy when she first got to the Ashram, but soon she opened up and became more confident and vocal and showed her leadership abilities.

Tara, Shanti, and Ila—and others—are the Maitreyians in "Kaivalya," the Center of our Holy Community, the Keepers of the Faith. We all have a fierceness in our devotion to Maitreya. We all have unwavering faith in Maitreya. Every one of us. This is the spiritual bond that holds us all together, forever, no matter what is going on in the material world.

Juana is a less experienced Maitreyian who I met years ago through office jobs, and then reconnected with later. She had that Midwestern, down-home essence that stood out in L.A. She was happy that she was able to meet Maitreya and come to sanctuary meditations and other events in the 1990's. She moved away, but came back after Maitreya passed away, and received Holy Initiation in 2013. She never seemed to have doubt about Maitreya but she, like most of us, goes through some personal obstacles at times. Like Shanti, she is sociable and sweet natured. Unlike Shanti, she (self-admittedly) cares too much about what other people think. I also see that trait of caring too much about what other people think in myself, but I try to work on my flaws. She doesn't have years of experience like us, but she shared some special experiences of Maitreya with me alongside her.

One memory I have of Juana is when we were doing Inner Divine Communion together while she was visiting here, sitting on my couch in Redondo Beach around 2016. I was wondering how Maitreya was in the hearts and souls of everyone, "all the time, all at once" and it ultimately made me question, how? How could he help me, and at the same time always be helping all Souls? Doesn't he need to do one-thing at a time? It was hard for my mind to grasp how he is with everyone at the same time. I felt bad taking Maitreya's time when he had so many souls to help simultaneously.

While Juana and I were sitting there, side-by-side, I felt a whoosh and I literally pulled my face back, like someone had just put their face right in front of mine; not unpleasant, just surprising. I pulled back because I could feel Maitreya right there! I saw a flash of his face. It was sweet, funny, and amazing all at the same time. He was right there. Juana, at the same moment, also pulled her head back. We both knew at the same instant that he was with us. She also saw him as I did, briefly. This experience was more external than the internal experiences I usually had. He was THERE in both of our faces. Letting us know: he can be with both of us at the exact same time. It finally made sense. I understood how Maitreya could be with all souls, all at the exact same time.

Another experience happened with us on Facetime. As we were ending our Inner Divine Communion Meditation, we both heard Maitreya loudly chanting, "*Ommmm*" in a deep, beautiful tone. I hadn't mentioned it yet when Juana asked, "*Did you hear Maitreya?*" Another wondrous experience among many.

One thing is certain. Every one of us—and other spiritual brothers and sisters not named here—have an unwavering faith in common. We have an unbroken distinctly-felt forever Spiritual Bond. Some of us don't even know each other, a few thousand awakened souls across the world, but we all have the Friend of all Souls in our hearts and minds and walking beside us and that commonality will hold us together, and we will bring changes to a suffering world.

One thing I would say to anyone learning my story is, *"Don't do what I did. Don't hold on to resentments and cause disharmony, especially when you have access to so many profound spiritual tools."*

We all hold fast to our deep devotion to Maitreya the Friend of All Souls, and we all have that in common. I may stand alone as the one who left, and came back, so many times, but I always came back, with my unwavering Faith and the knowledge that I am meant to follow Maitreya, forever.

No matter what struggle and strife I either went through, or more often caused myself, I never forsook my bond with Maitreya, the True Friend of All Souls; the one who taught me actual supreme Universal Love, the one who took me back with True Forgiveness, the one who showed constant sacrifice for the sake of others, and the one sent by Universal God for the sake of all suffering souls.

And if I did not endure suffering, how could I empathize with those who still do?

If I did not struggle, how could I help others in their struggles?

If I did not come to Know my True Self, how could I convince others to find out this Blissful Truth for themselves?

CHAPTER TEN

⤙⤙

"Celebrities"

A s Monty Python would say, "Now for something completely different." I've never put much stock in celebrities. Maitreya always used to say celebrity doesn't mean much of anything, since we are all One in Spirit. Nevertheless, I do find my celebrity sightings noteworthy because celebrities are an interesting topic and most people are familiar with them. And, more importantly, I sincerely wonder if God was putting me in their presence for Spiritual Contact, since they had various levels of worldly influences and (some) would make great conduits for Maitreya's teachings. And so, on a more material note, I now describe some of these chance, or perhaps fated, encounters.

Back in New Jersey in the 1970's:

I met author Kurt Vonnegut at an autograph signing with some local DJs.

I hung out with Southside Johnny and all the Jukes in Asbury Park and they all signed a *Welcome to Asbury Park* postcard that I had.

I talked with Meatloaf at a record store signing and I thought he was a very nice guy.

I had the opportunity to meet Iggy Pop at a similar radio station meet-and-greet, and he wrote, "*Keep Warm.*" I wondered if that was what he said to everyone, or if perhaps it was simply cold out. I like to imagine it meant he thought I had a warm personality, which would be a little off, but I was young at the time, so maybe.

In San Francisco in the 1980's:

I knew Chris Isaac fairly well in San Francisco for a few years in the mid through late 1980's. This is different from the other brief encounters. My ex-husband was a drummer in San Francisco and played with Chris quite a few times. They became good friends. At a party, I interrupted Isaac while he was singing and playing his guitar, and exclaimed *"You're going to be famous one day."* I had a strong flash of insight into the future, as would happen to me from time to time. He just smiled and nodded. He was very laid back. Once I had a birthday party for my husband (I think his 25th birthday) at our apartment. I wanted to invite couples for a "grown up" dinner party and so I only invited four couples. Chris Isaac and his girlfriend were the only ones who showed up! The four of us had a lovely time, but I was a little embarrassed that the party turned out to be so small.

I later met up with him at a club as he was just becoming well-known, at the start of it all. He said "of course" he remembered me. I asked what it was like to become famous and he just commented, "I still do my own laundry." I gave him a small copy of Maitreya's Destiny book. He commented, "I like how I can keep it in my shirt pocket."

Presently, after he's had so many years of success and so many people have come and gone, I doubt he'd know who I am; although, perhaps he could be reminded. What's more important is that I hope he knows or will know who Maitreya is.

Another significant celebrity-type relationship was a bond with Etta James. I socialized with Etta on quite a few occasions in the mid-1980s. I spent a significant amount of time talking with her on the phone over the course of a few years. I later read in a biography, that the years I knew her were considered "her darker years." Her career was in a slump. I worked part-time for her manager Lupe DeLeon while I was a student at San Francisco State University. Etta and I were friendly and had a good rapport. She would occasionally call in distress, and I would run to the Western Union to wire her money, often out of my own account when Lupe was not around. I did coke once with her and the band. Cocaine was definitely not a habit of mine, at all, but I felt at the time, perhaps foolishly, that this was an opportunity not to be missed. I spoke on the phone with her quite often and she was always sweet. We would chat while she talked about her sons, and her husband; she was very close to them. I seem to remember she did not like living in Los Angeles at that time. Unfortunately looking back, I wonder if my friendly contact was also possibly an unknowing enabler—but I was young and thought if this wonderful person needed money, well I'd send her some.

I also had several phone calls one day with Ron Wood who wanted Etta's phone number when she was in a minor car accident. I wouldn't give it to him, and he was quite upset with me. I remember a lot of "*Do you know who I am?*" and me being not quite sure. My husband loved the Rolling Stones but I wasn't sure if Ron Wood was in our favorite band or if he was from Rod Stewart's band (I figured out later, it was both). But I don't know why, I just didn't think I should give out phone numbers. Lupe finally gave him Etta's number when he came into the office and he had a good laugh that I wouldn't give it to Ron.

As grim as it sounds, one of my favorite experiences with Etta was years later at her funeral in January 2012. [That year 2012 was a huge year for loss. That's the same year I would go on to lose my mom in April, and of course the unforeseen devastating passing of Maitreya himself later that year in July.]

However, even in the darkest moments you can still find the light, and as I communed with Etta next to her coffin, I was filled with Universal Love and Compassion. She and I had birthdays near each other in late January. She almost made it to her birthday and it was actually my birthday when I went to her service (which became an amazing concert with Stevie Wonder and Christina Aguilera).

I felt, and knew, that she had accepted Maitreya's Initiation after I offered to her in Spirit. She sent me Love in return, so that I would know she accepted this Gift. I became completely immersed in an intense wave of love and bliss for about a minute. It was deeply poignant. There's a photo that an L.A. Times reporter took and emailed to me, showing me in front of her casket. Little did this reporter know that even though Etta had just passed, the picture they took captured one of the most profound moments between us. At least this is one "celebrity" who received Holy Initiation.

At that same job as assistant to the booking agent back in the early to mid-1980's, we were scheduling tours for James Brown. One day, Mr. Brown himself called—all day. It was just me in the office. I didn't know where Lupe was. James Brown called about ten or more times asking for him. We didn't say much but I remember us joking around a little, and hearing him do that well-known slow almost growling laughter a few times.

Now that I think about these early office experiences, it was a lot more *fun* when all we had were those regular land line telephones. No email, no cell phones, no texting, no social media, usually not even answering machines yet for when you weren't by the phone—although they arrived soon thereafter, along with fax machines. I got a raise because I went from typewriter to computer at that office, but it was a very basic Macintosh. The personal exchanges were much more memorable than the present-day digital attempts at communication.

In Los Angeles—1990's to Present

This next encounter was not in person. I did the Maitreyian Life Assistance Meditation, which is also a death-assistance if the person just left this world within previous days, for Kurt Cobain in 1994 after he committed suicide. I sat on the local beach and meditated and communicated with him spiritually. His anger and contempt were overwhelming. I took it personally and apologized that

I didn't reach out to him while he was alive. I'm still not sure what the onslaught of negativity was all about. Shortly afterward I posted to a live chat with Courtney Love on AOL and tried to tell her, but I don't know if she saw it.

On a more positive note, around 1992, I talked to Maureen Reagan, daughter of former President Ronald Reagan, at her campaign office in Torrance. I just walked right in, and went past the one other person in the front office. We chatted for at least twenty minutes, and she introduced me to her little dog. I was still a Democrat then, but told her I appreciated her father and the historical impact he had made. She gave me tickets to their campaign picnic nearby for the next day. Reagan himself was mere feet away from me giving a speech on stage while I was another foot away from the family as we sat on blankets in the park. It felt a bit surreal. At least she received Spiritual Contact (my strong intent the entire time we talked) before she passed away ten years later.

I encountered several other celebrities in L.A., including two occasions where I talked with Emilio Estevez. Once he was in a restaurant with Demi Moore, although she barely spoke. The more important aspect of that encounter, was that Maitreya himself talked a bit with them and I could see a bit of light in Emilo's eyes while meeting Maitreya. Then, around 1990, we had a much longer conversation while he was on break when filming near the police station in Redondo Beach. We sat on a wall and talked about spiritual and philosophical matters for quite a while—at least a half hour if not more. This was a special encounter as Emilio, who seemed sweet and deeply thoughtful, received more Spiritual Contact.

In contrast, an annoying occurrence happened after I briefly met a singer named Terence Trent D'Arby in the late 1990's. I noticed him in a limo that was stopped at a light with the window open. I only knew it was him because he just got into the car in front of the theater that had his name on the marquee. I was only vaguely familiar with his music. I thought I had a nice conversation with him, handed him a small version of the Holy Book of Destiny that we had at the time, and declined offers to party with them. (Someone else in the limo gave the offer to party.) Years later, around 2001, I saw an article indicating he changed his name to Maitreya! This blew my mind. We tried emailing him, but to no avail. He rudely insisted that his name change was completely unrelated to the book I'd given him, and that he could change his name to whatever he wanted. He has gone by Sananda Maitreya since then. I wish I had not talked to him; perhaps, he was an egotist long before we met.

I was introduced to attorney Leo Terrell for a brief conversation back in 1998 in the conference room at a law firm I was working at. He was liberal at the time. He is now conservative and, in my perspective, has seen the light politically. I believe his spiritual contact with Maitreya contributed to his transformation.

I attended Bill Maher's show at a small comedy club in Hermosa Beach years ago. I intentionally did one of our Spiritual Practices of strongly Flowing The Power to him, and now he sees the light and speaks truth, regardless of politics. Coincidence? Maybe. I'd like to think it's not just coincidence, but there's no way to know for sure. The only outward conversation was some joking about me being a legal assistant. He started with a silly joke, saying, "Oh, so you're of legal age, good," but quickly looked sheepish. It was part of some banter about where my niece Sarah and I were from. We had just stopped by on our way to the airport to drop her off. She was about 15 at the time so hopefully he wasn't referring to her, but maybe he was in an innocent manner.

Shanti and I crossed paths with some rappers who were filming nearby. I am not sure what year it was in the 90's, but I believe one of them was Ice Cube. We did meet Run DMC and they even mentioned Maitreya in one of their songs—more than that, they "sampled" one of his talks. As amazing as it was to hear a Run DMC lyric about Maitreya, with his teachings interspersed, I felt as if I was the only one who thought it was cool that Maitreya's voice was on a rap song. Not many others in our community shared my excitement.

I have a hard time finding this song now, so if anyone finds it, let me know.

A more on-going encounter started around 1990, when I lived next door to Ron Kovic, who wrote the book, *Born on the Fourth of July*, which was made into the movie starring Tom Cruise. I said hello to Ron a few times; one time he asked me if I was a singer. When I gave a surprised, "*No!?*" he mentioned that he heard me singing in the shower and thought I sounded pretty good. This cracked me up because I am practically tone deaf, but I guess I was letting loose when I thought nobody could hear. On the night I got back from seeing the movie in early 1990, I saw him in his window, sitting in his living room with the light on, so I went up and knocked on his door. He let me in and we sat and talked for about an hour. He autographed my paperback book and much later I noticed he had written his phone number at the end pages. I never did call him. (It's probably for the best that this was before cell phones so there was no texting.) I would just see him around. One day he was getting in his car and wrapped a scarf around him and asked me "how do I look?" I said he reminded me of a mobster John Gotti for some reason; still not sure why I said that but Ron seemed to appreciate it as an off-handed compliment. Whenever I would run into him for years after that, at grocery stores and coffee houses, which I still do occasionally, he'd say *"Yes, I remember you, you knocked on my door late at night!"* The last time was only a few months ago. Ron seems to be an intelligent, quiet, thoughtful person, but with an edge. I guess I'd have an edge, too, if I went through what he did. However, I believe he is somehow "in his own way," as far as obstacles in receiving Maitreya's Holy Initiation goes.

Also, in the early 1990's, we were all extras in Oliver Stone's movie, *The Doors*. It's fairly common for people who live in the Los Angeles area to have been an extra at one time or another. As a community, we thought it might be a good way to contact others. It really wasn't. It was mostly uncomfortable. We stood in a concert arena for hours. Some assistants threw sandwiches wrapped in plastic to us from the stage, like we were hungry animals. Val Kilmer basically ignored us but he was a good actor. I saw Billy Idol accidentally hit a female extra in the face when he threw a microphone in her direction. After all that, I did see the back of my head (my hair was distinctive) in the concert crowd when I watched the movie, but you had to look fast. I still hope that wasn't all a complete waste of time but I am not sure (I was the one who mentioned the possibility when I heard a radio ad). It was at a minimum a slight bonding experience for the Community ourselves.

It was around the late 90's when I visited a local radio personality, Jim Ladd at KLSX, at his studio, but he was a little rude. I do think he received Holy Initiation; although, I wonder if he understood it at the time, so that's a question mark. I listened to him for years though, as he had excellent taste in rock music.

I met Jesse Ventura when he was the Governor of Minnesota, who was a spokesperson for freedom that resonated with the Spiritual Community's beliefs. He was doing a book signing in L.A. in 2000. He seemed to be a cool guy.

On the flight on my way to see my Dad in 2002, which would turn out to be our last visit, I sat next to Tom Berenger. A kind coworker had a relative who worked for the airlines and they upgraded me to First Class to go back to New Jersey. Tom Berenger was one of the nicest people I ever met. He was reading a book about the Civil War and talked to me about it. He showed me photos of his wife and children. I actually fell asleep toward the end of the flight and my head was almost on his shoulder. He got a little uncomfortable but we laughed. (Later I made bad jokes that I had slept with Tom Berenger.) I believe he at least received Spiritual Contact. He is a kind soul. My Dad thought it was a somewhat interesting story when I visited him.

A highlight in 2011, I met one of Maitreya's favorite authors, the esteemed science fiction author Ray Bradbury. In one of Maitreya's favorite novels, Stranger in a Strange Land, the writer coined a term, "grok," which meant to grasp a concept on a deep level. Our community ended up borrowing this term and it became a deep-rooted saying in our vernacular. In the Spiritual Community, we all strongly identified with that novel, Stranger in a Strange Land since we were all—well, strangers in a strange land. On the occasion where we would all come to a collective understanding of something, we would say we "grokked it!" At the time I met him, Bradbury was in a wheelchair and I said something in reference to "grok." I'm not sure if he heard me, but he seemed sweet as he stared at me. Later, upon fact-checking amidst this book's creation, I realized my error. Ray Bradbury had, in fact, not written Stranger in a Strange Land, it was Robert A. Heinlein. I laugh at this realization, and now Bradbury's lack of response makes sense.

I ran into Larry King in Beverly Hills around 2011 but I couldn't get my phone camera to work. He seemed irritated as he posed, impatiently waiting by his car so I said, "*Never mind, have a nice day.*" He was a little grumpy. Or at least he was that day, and probably had to get somewhere while I was fiddling with my phone. In all encounters, I would quickly Call on Maitreya so that a minimum of Spiritual Contact occurred. But truly, I do that with all encounters of any kind of person at any moment.

I met with war-hero Louie Zamperini two or three times around 2011 in the South Bay area, his hometown. The first time was at an Unbroken book signing, where he signed, "*Be Hardy*" to me, and the second time was at the Torrance Armed Forces Parade. He laughed and smiled a lot and said something about my name sounding foreign. I could not get past some resistance when inviting him to be in the Redondo Beach Memorial Day Parade, but we had some sweet moments.

Shanti and I met all the members of the Moody Blues at a small venue nearby around 2010 or so. Their name, unfortunately, was fairly apt. They were certainly moody, rude, and snotty. I guess they were a bit perturbed that we were even there—after finding our way backstage. Shanti wanted to be nice to them because they were Maitreya's favorite band in the 60's and 70's, but as it turned out, Maitreya didn't like us chasing those so-called celebrities.

So, I wasn't the only one who encountered "famous" people, as Shanti also met several noteworthy people, including the day she and others went to Charlton Heston's home. They said he was extremely gracious and kind, came to the door himself, and talked with them as he accepted some booklets.

It was also memorable years earlier when Shanti spoke to concert promoter Bill Graham on the phone. He called her. She had written and basically said, "*If not you, who; if not now, when*" and—as he was often described as being perpetually in a state of anger—he fiercely chastised her that he had done plenty for others in this world. Only a few days later, he died in a helicopter crash. We made macabre comments about how she drove him to this, but we were a bit relieved that he had at least had Spiritual Contact before exiting this world.

Back to a chronological list, a highlight is when I spoke with Dolph Lungren at the UFC Gym in Torrance around 2015. He was mellow, kind and friendly. I'm not sure he understood my comments about how Maitreya liked his movies. He was respectful though, a nice down-to-earth guy. I was teased by friends later that I should have asked if he was single, because he was only a few years older than me. But of course, he ended up marrying the much younger, beautiful model type—what else, right? I am smiling as I relate that.

In November of 2018, I encountered Dennis Rodman at a book signing (with his agent, an intense but pleasant guy named Darren Prince) at The Grove in L.A. We exchanged books: I gave him our Holy Book of Destiny. He has received Spiritual Contact. There was some controversy at the time because he had spoken to Korean dictator Kim Jon Un about basketball and life. I didn't judge that as harshly—getting to the heart of humanity with anyone in power is not a bad thing in my view.

I'm supposedly just one person away from Elon Musk, but nothing ever happens. The engineer who lives in the unit below mine works for SpaceX. She barely talks to anyone, including me, which isn't personal—she's just introverted. Although I like to imagine to myself that she's doing top-secret stuff, and that's why she keeps to herself. I asked her if working at SpaceX means knowing Elon personally. She said, "Oh, I talk to him all the time. We have meetings in person on a regular basis, and we're on the phone every week." I've actually heard some zoom calls—I can't hear much of what they say, and even if I could, I doubt I'd understand it all.

And, for perhaps the most controversial newsworthy individual I had contact with—whatever side of the news you might watch—Donald Trump.

Before my encounter with Donald Trump, an employer of mine was in a legal battle with him and, truthfully, I thought Trump was in the right—at least of his opinion of this employer. He and my former employer went back and forth with name calling and mudslinging, as legal battles often go. To my delight, the local paper ran a story that quoted Trump saying this lawyer was an ass, and I thought he was right in that opinion. (I thought it quite funny that these two big egos were calling each other names.) After I had left my employment (he now holds a lot of legal power as a Judge so you can understand why his name has been redacted), I sent Donald Trump's office a fax in which I voiced my support for Trump's characterization of this ex-employer. Around February of 2005, I had a voice mail message on my home answering machine (yes kids, that's what we had back then) saying, *"This is Donald Trump's office, please call"*—with a New York number. I didn't even call back right away. Then while at work, a call came in on my new cell phone (which was very high-tech at the time) where a young woman said, *"Is this Shraddha? Please hold for Donald Trump."* I was a bit shocked, as I didn't anticipate that he would actually pay attention to the letter I had faxed, never mind contact me directly. At that time, he was also known for his fairly new TV show "The Apprentice." I immediately had no doubt I was hearing his unique voice.

Our conversation was originally about the letter I had sent and in response Donald Trump asked for more information about my ex-employer that, unfortunately, I didn't have. I think he thought I was playing hardball so he kept repeating, *"I'll indemnify you; I'll indemnify you."* He was quite the character. Although the purpose of his call seemed to be legal matters, after we had settled that topic he suddenly asked about my name, *"Shraddha, that's an unusual name."* He asked what it meant, who gave it to me and of course that transgressed into a conversation about Maitreya and our community. He specifically asked, *"What is your main belief?"* I pared it down to *"We are all One in Spirit,"* and the more questions he had, I was eager to answer. I mean, at the time he wasn't a politician yet but he was still Donald Trump and he was showing a surprising amount of interest in a random legal assistant's faith and beliefs—must be a sign, right? We ended up having a wonderful conversation and I flowed the Power for Good from Maitreya and Universal God to him throughout the phone call. A coworker said it sounded like we were old friends after a 20-minute call.

A few years later, while assisting Maitreya with the local Memorial Day parade he created, I contacted Trump's office in New York again. His assistant directed me to the appropriate person at the local Trump National Golf Club. Maitreya was organizing the first Navy Ship to visit Redondo Beach. I was told that Trump himself instructed the Golf Club organization to make sure the Navy guys got whatever they needed—they later said they thoroughly enjoyed the free passes to a beautiful day on the links. During our efforts to arrange this day for the crew, some attorneys I worked for explained to me that the course caused a lot of golf balls to get lost, since it's on the side of an ocean cliff. After the event, there was a cocktail meet and greet at the Marina where Maitreya introduced me to the Captain of the ship. He exclaimed how wonderful the golf game was and I blurted out, *"I heard you need to have a lot of balls to play there!"* I was referencing the geographical issues of the golf course, but they didn't know that. There was a moment of shock on the Captain's face, and a brief sheepish look from me while my sentence hung in the air, and then we all burst out laughing—Maitreya, the Captain, the Navy guys around him, and myself.

Did I lose you, dear reader? In my efforts to share my encounters with Donald Trump, I ultimately just want to draw attention to the "wow" of it all. Currently as I write this, the division in our country is appalling. But who would have thought me of all people (a Maitreyian) would have spoken to, and been affected by, the now two-times elected President of the United States? His combination of heart and love for our country, his ego, and abrasiveness might be seen by some as inappropriate, unprofessional, and unpresidential. However, no matter who you are, you could likely agree that to continue with the cookie-cutter politicians was not, and will not, get us anywhere. After all, many people including Maitreya describe insanity as doing the same thing over and over while still expecting different results. And perhaps some of us forgot the basic concept: It is not who's right, but what's right.

I am a bit of an underdog, an imperfect person, and an imperfect disciple but I believe I have the power to make change—this is why I am writing this. I had thought maybe this country needs an underdog too, someone whose career has not been built off politics but rather business. Unfortunately, the current division in our society is still ongoing. Good people are almost seemingly living in completely different realities. (To me, one reason is either a person gets immersed in media propaganda, or they instead follow their heart and look for truth.) This is part of the same division that Maitreya and all of God's Awakened Ones have come here to heal.

It is interesting that his detractors keep doomsaying that Trump will cause war, and yet he keeps proving to be the one who avoids wars. As of this writing, he even recently destroyed Iran's nuclear capability. Don't get me wrong—I experienced the societal fear. I was quite nervous for a day or two until I realized he once again did the right thing—and moderate Democrats agreed.

But Maitreya often said, we will not change the world with politics—we can only truly change the world spiritually. And that spiritual awakening will then bring about the worldly and political changes.

Time to stop this oversimplified nonsense of choosing colors and sides, red or blue, like the old days in Los Angeles gangs where they had to be either Crips or Bloods. Time to just be Americans and choose what is truly best for America, no matter what propaganda is currently being pushed out by the powers that be. (Yes, I realize I still get too strident in my older age. All I can say is if that bothers you, you are blessed you didn't encounter me in my younger days.) But these encounters with Trump were the epitome of material-world cultural events in my life. I have reservations about both political extremes and often pray our country prioritizes truth above all else.

There were other brief encounters in my life (at least 20) with so-called famous people—just moments with Richard Dreyfuss, Robin Williams, Ginger Baker, Chuck Berry, Stan Lee, Bobcat Goldthwait, Mario Savio (all in San Francisco area) and, Tom Waits, Crispin Glover, Aaron Spelling, Corey Feldman, Leo DiCaprio (just for a minute); others in L.A. area). One opportunity I regret—Tom Hanks was filming a movie nearby at the same time as Leonardo DiCaprio (it was called "Catch Me if You Can"). My neighbor said, "He's right there in the trailer across the street." But I would grapple with the feeling of Maitreya not wanting any "chasing," although I literally just needed to walk across the street and say "hi." There were other missed opportunities since there is often filming around here—but if it gets too difficult, I just give up. Or I settle on the truth that "celebrities" are just people, just souls like anyone else.

I do hope, actually believe, that Maitreya "used me" which is in keeping with my ongoing intention to do so, for him to reach each soul I encounter—whether their reputations are well known or in smaller circles, it doesn't really matter. As long as the spiritual contact is for the good of all, I am happy to attempt to be his instrument of enlightenment. Perhaps it's my Catholic background, but I always loved St. Francis of Assisi Prayer for Peace, *make me an instrument of your peace, where there is hatred let me sow love... where there is doubt, faith.* I don't always succeed with love, but I have triumphed in faith.

It is safe to say I've crossed paths with many well-known personalities over the years, from actors, authors, musicians, and politicians, and I do hope there were some spiritual reasons behind it all.

But celebrity is fleeting. I hope my meetings or even moments with powerful and influential people have been used as a vessel in which to share and spread our message of The Friend's gift of Enlightenment and way to Self-Realization.

Because still, the greatest, most important person I will ever meet over many years, is and always will be, Maitreya, the Friend of All Souls.

Etta James funeral 2012

Dennis Rodman

CHAPTER ELEVEN

My Name Means Faith

Even today, years after his physical death, I still see The Friend, Maitreya. In early July of 2022 I was feeling down, so I did what I usually do when I need to take a break and recoup from whatever I'm going through: I meditated. In my meditation, I spoke with Maitreya. He reminded me, "*Do not forget that you are named Shraddha. It means to 'have faith.'*"

This caused me to contemplate how "Shraddha" doesn't just mean faith, it means the difference between blind faith, and faith through experience. From the moment I met him, I never lost my faith in Maitreya. At first my faith in him may be judged as blind, but I instantly trusted this man, and sensed something about him. We had a connection, but that was basically all I knew up until that point. Over time though, my faith grew stronger. After seeing firsthand how Maitreya led us and healed so many souls, my faith became rooted in experience. I can't even imagine having doubts now. Not about who Maitreya was (and is), nor about why he was here. What I know, I know. I've had unwavering faith.

I have faith that others will gain their own true faith through their own direct experience too. I don't expect people to believe out of nowhere or just because I said so. But it's a real mind-bender when I see people receive experiences from Maitreya The Friend and yet still not attribute or credit this enlightenment to him. They look around and give credit elsewhere. Just another example of this Age of Kali Yuga; darkness messing with us.

It's a little bit funny, when I first received my name, I wasn't a fan. We have "Tara," which means Mother Earth. We have "Ila" which means Spreader of the Light. And of course there is "Shanti" which means Peace. And many others. But when I first heard the name, "Shraddha," it sounded harsh. It wasn't light and sweet, like the other names. It was heavy and stern.

But I quickly told my family that I had a new name. My declaration was not received well. My father did not call me Shraddha for many years. At one time he put together old family movies into videos and narrated over it. Whenever I was in a scene, there was silence. He didn't know what to call me. I realized this years later and wished he had just asked me. I would have assured him that calling me my "old" family name on the videos would have been fine. One of my brothers also insisted on writing "Faith" on cards he sent to me instead of "Shraddha." That was fine with me. I was just happy he was thinking of me at all.

Shanti herself also reminded me several times over the years, "*Remember, 'Shraddha' means Faith,*" and she would say it, text it, or email it, at the exact right moment that I needed to hear it.

Over time I grew proud of the meaning behind the name. I'm proud that my name says something about the strength of my faith.

It's been the faith that I have in myself that I've been weakest in. All these questions live in my head: Am I going to make sense? Am I going to put important words together and make the right impact? Am I going to stop insulting people? Am I going to stop saying the wrong things at the wrong time and do more things that are right?

Sometimes I *do* say that right thing, at the right time, and make the impact I want. When that happens, I know it's Universal God and The Friend guiding me. When I am truly open and ready to receive Divine Guidance, Maitreya is with me, and I say what is right to be spoken, when it is right to be spoken.

A few days after my meditation session when Maitreya reminded me of the meaning behind my name, a few worldly validations happened that stuck with me. My friend Deb was staying with me and it wasn't going too well. I was having insomnia and she was having anxiety. Not a great combination for two people sharing one small space. But, one silver lining of the visit is when Deb said, "*I must tell you my realization: that Shraddha means Faith and you've always...had faith. You have never lost it. Not ever. No matter what your situation in your spiritual community was, you've held fast.*" And that meant the world to me. As somebody who's always so unsure, always second guessing myself, to have a friend unknowingly validate exactly what I was unsure of, felt like just what I needed. And to hear it, just days after my Meditation with Maitreya which I had not mentioned to her, was amazing.

The amazement didn't stop there. Just a few days later, a yoga teacher and friend of mine who is also named Debbie, texted me and let me know, "*During a yoga class today, I realized Shraddha means 'FAITH!'*" She texted that in all caps.

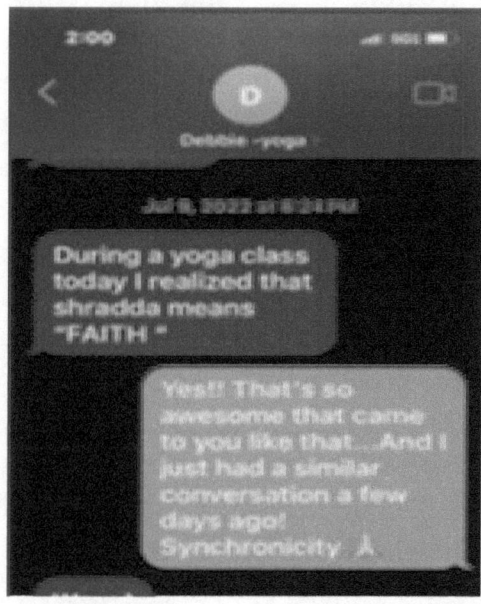

These two events happened within days of each other, shortly after my communication with The Friend. I love that about him. Even from the spiritual realm, he's looking out for me. He wants me to know that he recognizes how steadfast I can be, even in the face of uncertainty.

Faith is something that's integral to everything we do as a Community. It is a part of our way of life to ask for and receive Guidance, even on the smaller things in life, like what direction to walk in or where to drive. It's something we can all do. And sure enough, I have encountered people that I've transmitted spiritual assistance to whether they were aware of it or not, after receiving such Guidance from God and The Friend.

We don't even pray in the traditional sense of asking God for specifics. That's not how we see the Flowing Kijai, the Power for Good that Can Do No Wrong. It's a way of life. We don't believe in dictating what course of actions the universe manifests. As we like to say, organizations that "pray" often "prey" on people when nobody's watching.

Instead of praying, we leave it up to each soul—and God—what Kijai is used for, wherever needed and whatever the choice is used for. That's one more thing I love about the Maitreyians. Unlike most other religions, faith doesn't flow in just one direction. We don't blindly have faith in some higher power to make all our decisions for us, and we don't pray in a request or two to make the path easier for us. Instead, the faith flows forwards and backwards, up, and down. We have faith in God to choose the right path for everybody, but we also have faith in each individual soul to walk that path, and make the right choices along the way. Most of all, we have faith that we will find the people who are right and ready to become true Maitreyians—and bring this supreme Faith through direct experience to each willing Soul.

I may not be able to see the end of our Mission in this lifetime—complete Divine Critical Mass for the sake of All Souls—but maybe at least I will see the beginning of it. Maitreya tragically should have seen more spiritual success while in this lifetime, but at least he will know in the Spiritual Realm that his Self-Sacrifices will come to fruition.

Maitreya's giving up Perfect Final Union to come back for others can be illustrated by a few very simplistic ideas that serve only as a glimpse of the big picture: it is like being snuggled up in bed, in bliss, but forcing yourself to get up into the cold to help other people, forever. It is like winning a huge lottery, and giving away every cent of it, keeping none of it for yourself, to give it to others in the world. It is like being at the head of a line, and then opening the door, standing behind it, and letting every single Soul go before you: to Perfect Union with God; while you wait for them all to pass before you. These are simple examples to be multiplied a thousand times, to exemplify Maitreya's pure Love and Self-Sacrifice for the sake of all others.

Spiritual Love

Among so many lessons, the lesson of direct experience of what real Love is—real true Universal Spiritual Love—is one of the most impactful to me. I've expanded from not feeling love at all, to barely feeling it in some relationships, to an absolute limitless supreme Love that goes beyond just feelings, for all Beings. I practice Universal Love for all Souls apart from the acts of the body it inhabits. I can disagree with and even hate some actions, but still love the same Spirit of God which is within us all. I truly practice one of our first principles which says, to See God in All, and All in God.

Practice is the word because it is a constant learning and growing experience until the day I leave this material world.

One of the more difficult practices of Universal Love, for me, is the expectation to love *yourself* even as you love the One Universal God. I had to work on loving myself—almost (although not quite) even more than I had to work on loving people who chose evil in the world. I know and practice that no man or woman is our enemy; the Force of Darkness alone is our enemy. Our only weapon is the Sharp Sword of Universal God's Pure Divine Truth. As Maitreya taught, we recognize and insist upon the inherent and inalienable Dignity and Worth of each Soul apart from the acts of the body that it inhabits. I could practice that principle toward evil people, but yet still have a hard time accepting and loving my own self.

I do, now, love who I have become and who I will continue to become. I love my True highest Self, because of true Faith, gained through experience through God's Grace. I know who I truly am at my essence, how I got to be where I am, and the pureness of my heart and intentions.

The deep love I felt for Maitreya was instantaneous and grew deeper and spread to all around me and to all humanity, the more years I followed him. And, although I have led a fairly isolated life compared to most people, I literally have never walked alone since my Holy Initiation. Maitreya is always with me.

This intense real Love is one of the gifts in Spirit that Maitreya gave to me. Shortly after Maitreya left this physical world, on 12th of Service 60 AF (August 12, 2012) I had been wondering if Maitreya is feeling anything now that He is in the Spiritual Realm. I suddenly had an overwhelming sense of my entire Being, completely immersed in Love. It was a big, Universal Love. It was the kind of love I only had a few glimpses of Pure Bliss in various meditations and Darshans with Maitreya over the years.

I look across the bedroom into the living room. I see an outline of Maitreya standing there near my bookcase! This also happens to be near some of his ashes. I know he is there! I am filled with a piercing Love, not just coming from within me, but being Given to me by Maitreya. I asked him, "Is this where you are all the Time now, in this Love for All Beings?" He answered, "Yes." He gives me a Knowing-ness—I feel a deep love and compassion for all Souls where He is now.

This wasn't just his universal love, though. This encounter was quite personal. This unconditional love continued on a deeply personal level. He enveloped me in a wave of pure real love, even from beyond this physical world, perhaps so I would remember what love really is.

I was later reminded of the stories of The Disciples seeing Jesus appear to them after he died to this world, and knew I just had a similar experience. Maitreya had literally just appeared to me shortly after leaving this world!

I now reflect how, over the years, my heart was often like thin paper, easily cut. And because of these cuts I lashed out on those around me. Maitreya and the Community's flames of Truth would sometimes burn my paper heart. But then their Pure Light and Love would shower me with unending Faith and Forgiveness.

No regrets can stand the test of time, but being washed in both Universal God and Maitreya's Clear Divine Love remain forever in my Soul.

I raged, I damaged, I disrupted. But I faced the consequences and always grew stronger in Faith. I will never be able to repay Maitreya and my spiritual brothers and sisters for all their love and forgiveness, but I promise that my unwavering Faith will be a Light for others in this dark world. I want to bring them to Maitreya, the Friend of All Souls.

Maitreya taught me and showered me with a deep profound Universal Love, in this world and from beyond it. I am forever changed. I am no longer self-loathing and withdrawn. My bruised heart is no longer calloused. I am filled with the greatest of Love for all Humanity, forever.

I am Faith through experience. I am Faith. I am Shraddha.

Epilogue

When waiters and waitresses would ask Maitreya, "*Is there any-thing else I can get for you,*" he would sometimes reply, "*Just a few more minutes at the end of my life.*" Although it was a surprising statement, everyone would laugh. But after he passed into the Spiritual Realm, I often wished for all those minutes. So, I will use my own last minutes here, to try to reach the right people through this memoir.

I do not have a happy ending here. I do not have the achievement and resolution of finally creating Divine Critical Mass in the World. But I can get the word out. I am now an older woman who vowed years ago to save the world and has yet barely managed to save myself. It also took me several years just to put this memoir together.

And so, dear reader, I leave you with this: if I could take this journey, so could you. If I could truly experience my True Self as One with the One Universal God, so can you. If I can help others, so can you. If I could become truly Spiritually Enlightened and well on my way toward Self-Realization, believe me, so can anyone who opens their heart and does this spiritual work that any motivated person can do.

If I, as a somewhat damaged person, can truly experience One-ness with God, and give Maitreya's Gift to others, so can you. It doesn't matter if you've been a seeker for years. It doesn't matter if you happened to read this on a whim. You can do this. Be a Truth Seeker and a Truth Finder.

But we don't do this just for ourselves. There is a war between good and evil going on in our world—right now. Help God win. Help *Good* win. There will ultimately be the Victory of Good over Evil. But, how long will that take? It is completely dependent on all of our Free Will! Some Christians are saying they "want the Rapture" now. To me, this is similar to Muslims who "want Jihad." How about, instead, all good people come together and combine our goodness and Free Will to defeat the evil in this world—and restore Universal God's Truth—to all religions?

This is urgent. It is not enough for us to just become enlightened ourselves. It is necessary to truly save humanity from self-destruction. We can reach Divine Critical Mass, when a certain portion of the world's population receives the Friend's Holy Initiation and follows him to Oneness with God. We will spiritually save the world in a real and profound way.

If you're still not sure, why not try anyway? What is the harm in doing good in the world and tipping the scale toward Full Enlightenment? Why not help bring the Truth back to all religions? Why not help people follow their religions in their purity, instead of living in a world of untruths? People can truly worship all Founders of true religions in a Spirit of real love, instead of based on fear. Stop the Fear. Love God, do not Fear God. Love one another, do not live in Fear. But, if you are afraid sometimes, go forward in spite of it. Maitreya taught that Courage is moving forward despite fear—and then fears are usually conquered. There is no need to fear death of the body (trust me, I know that one is not easy). Fear instead, wasting life while we have it—and use that as a motivating factor while here. As Maitreya said, *"Fear is the enemy. God is the remedy."*

The more I came to know my True Self as Spirit, the fewer fears I had in daily life, except for basic survival fears.

Maitreya is here for you.

An acquaintance recently mentioned "False Idols" or "False Prophets." I wondered, why not take *that* literally, as other things in the Bible are taken literally. What is false here? Nothing. What idols are here? None. What prophets am I speaking of? None.

No need to only take my word here. For example, whenever I wasn't able to be in Maitreya's presence, I could look at any photo of him and concentrate on him and merge in spirit with him at that moment. He had done this exercise himself when he attended martial arts classes. He would gaze intently at the master's photo adorning the wall, allowing himself to connect with the founder's spirit before embracing the guidance of the teacher in class. One of our brothers performed "Darshan," this dwelling on Maitreya, while in the military in Afghanistan, and he was the only soldier in his troop who was never injured.

Whenever I gaze and focus on Maitreya, I transcend material world angst and know who I truly Am—I am Spirit which is One with Universal Spirit. I ask that you take a moment and look, truly spiritually gaze, at any photo of Maitreya with the Intention to call on him and dwell upon his and God's Presence. Even if a person's Faith is only for a few minutes of experimentation, they can know the Truth.

You too can attain Faith Through Direct Experience.

Photo of Maitreya The Friend of All Souls, apx. 1987

Maitreya's Promise:

"Whosoever among you believes in me and calls upon me as one of my Faithful, holding my Presence within your mind, and calling out within your heart, 'Bhagavan Ji! Bhagavan Ji! Bhagavan Ji" Unto you I will come; and within you I will abide, guiding you ever closer to the Infinite and Eternal Bliss of Perfect Union with God; and you will never walk alone."

As Maitreya said:

"*God's Eternal Universal Religion is not a replacement for or a negation or contradiction of the other Religions that have been established by God's Mercies to Man. Neither is The Friend of all Souls a replacement for or a negation or contradiction of the many Mercies God has sent unto Man. To the contrary, The Friend is a living extension and affirmation of all of the Prophets, Saints, Buddhas, Saviors and Avataras as God has sent to Man throughout the Ages and God's Eternal Universal Religion is an extension and affirmation of all of the earlier Religions they gave unto Man. In every age, when humanity has fallen into materialism and darkness rules the land, God sends forth his Mercies to Man in such ways and in such measure as are best suited to the times and needs of Man. The Friend is God's Mercy to Man in this age. God's Eternal Universal Religion is the Religion God has sent The Friend forth into this world to establish, to save Man from total self-destruction and spread God's Universal Salvation and Liberation to all Souls everywhere.*" (Adhyatma Bhagavan The Friend, 6/29/2001.)

By The Will and Grace of The One Universal God: From the Holy Book of Destiny

"*Go out into the darkness of this world and light up The Divine Fire of the Spirit of God within the hearts of all Beings. Go out into the desert of this World and give The Holy Water of Life of this New Covenant, unto all who thirst after The Truth; that he who has eyes may See; and he who has ears may Hear; and they shall know within their hearts The Truth of This Truth. For, whosoever shares The Water of Life shares The One Universal God and The Friend. Of this there is no doubt!*"

"*Gather together My Faithful of all Nations into My Holy Community, that this, which is The Word of That I AM THAT I AM shall cover the Earth from Sun to Sun. To the end that all Souls shall receive your Holy Initiation; that they who follow you to the end of this life shall win, thereby, The Supreme Gift of Liberation and Perfect Final Union with The One God, That One Universal I AM THAT I AM, which your Supreme Self-Sacrifice has won for all Souls."*

The Friend of All Souls, Maitreya.
The Holy Book of Destiny (p. 124). Kindle Edition.

We are Soldiers of The Light. Our one Purpose and Mission in this world is to defeat The Force of Darkness with the Sharp Sword of Universal God's Pure Divine Truth; end The Age of Ignorance, Darkness, Chaos, Confusion, Delusion, Illusion and Destruction; restore God's Eternal Universal Religion to all the peoples of the Earth; and bring The Age of Universal God's Pure Divine Truth into fullness and Reality for the continued survival of Humanity and the Salvation and Liberation of all Souls for all time; that all Souls may attain Perfect Final Union with God at the end of this life and be set free, forever.

The Friend of All Souls, Maitreya.
The Holy Book of Destiny (p. 9). Kindle Edition.

You may obtain your own copy of Maitreya the Friend of All Souls, Holy Book of Destiny, available on Amazon. The method of Inner Divine Communion is in The Holy Book of Destiny.

My friends, I leave you with this.

May the Peace and Love of the One Universal God and Maitreya the Friend of All Souls be with you and yours always.

And, most of all, may your Faith become as strong, or even stronger, than my own.

With true Universal Love,
Shraddha
("Faith Through Experience")

Maitreya's Prayer of Divine Victory
(Evening last Prayer)

O Paratpara! Beloved Universal God of Countless Names and Forms who art beyond all Names and Forms! Beloved I AM THAT I AM! Thou alone art my One True Self! Through Thy Holy Initiation Thou hast revealed my Oneness with Thee! I surrender completely unto Thee!

Thy Authority is restored! Thy Presence has become manifest within this little self! I shine forth by Thy Divine Clear Light! The division in me is Healed! I know my Oneness with Thee! I know Thy Oneness in all this that is! All is made Perfect! I lack for nothing!

Thou hast consumed my Ignorance in The Sacred Fire of Thy Presence. Thou hast led me through the Ordeal! Through Thy Holy Initiation, Thou hast revealed my Oneness with Thee; and liberated me from the endless rounds of birth and death!

From the unreal, Thou hast led me to The Real!

From darkness, Thou hast led me to The Light!

From division, Thou hast led me to Wholeness!

From the temporary, Thou hast led me to The Eternal!

From death, Thou hast led me to Immortality!

O Beloved Universal One! I am One with Thee this moment!

My Doing is One with my Speech!

My Speech is One with my Mind!

Mind is One with my Heart!

My Heart is One with my Will!

And my Will is One with Thy Will!

Thou hast shattered my prison of false self; and absorbed me, in The Ocean of Thy Infinite Divine Being; like a drop of water in The Sea!

I know, without doubt or reservation that Thee and I are not we, but One! That which Thou Art, I Am!

Thou art my Only True Self; Majestic! Splendorous! Immortal!

There is no I but Thee! So is it with me!

Om So'ham tat tvam asi! I Am That, Thou Art That! Jai Bhagavan Ji! Victory To That Beloved Universal I AM THAT I AM Which Thou Art!

The Friend of All Souls, Maitreya.
The Holy Book of Destiny (pp. 195-196). Kindle Edition.

Before my time—Maitreyians apx. 1977

Maitreya and me (earlier 1990's and then apx. 2003)

Spiritual Sisters apx 2013

Maitreyian Family apx 2013

Maitreya The Friend of All Souls—Spiritual Revolutionary photo apx. 1980

Founder of God's Eternal Universal Religion
"The Holy Book of Destiny"
Maitreyathefriend.com